Coming Home

Coming Home

A Theology of Housing

Edited by Malcolm Brown and
Graham Tomlin

CHURCH HOUSE
PUBLISHING

Church House Publishing
Church House
Great Smith Street
London SW1P 3AZ

ISBN 978 1 78140 188 0

Published 2020 by Church House Publishing

The opinions expressed in this book are those of the authors and do
not necessarily reflect the official policy of the General Synod or The
Archbishops' Council of the Church of England.

Scripture quotations are from the following versions of the Bible:
Chapters 1, 8, 9 and 10: HOLY BIBLE, NEW INTERNATIONAL
VERSION. Copyright © 1973, 1978, 1984, 2011 by Biblica, Inc.
Used by permission of Zondervan. All rights to be reserved worldwide.
Chapter 1: The Message. Copyright © 1993, 1994, 1995, 1996, 2000,
2001, 2002. Used by permission of NavPress Publishing Group.
Chapters 2, 4, 5, 7 and 8: New Revised Standard Version Bible:
Anglicized Edition. Copyright © 1989, 1995 National Council of
the Churches of Christ in the United States of America. Used by
permission. All rights reserved worldwide.
Chapter 3: ESV Bible (The Holy Bible, English Standard Version).
Copyright © 2001 by Crossway, a publishing ministry of Good News
Publishers. Used by permission. All rights reserved.

British Library Cataloguing in Publication data

A catalogue record for this book is available from the British Library

Printed and bound in England by
CPI Group (UK) Ltd

Contents

About the Contributors

Stephen Backhouse is a political theologian. He is the author of several books and articles on religious nationalism, church history and the work of Søren Kierkegaard. He has been Lecturer in Social and Political Theology for St Mellitus College and Dean of Westminster Theological Centre. Currently he is the director of Tent Theology.

Malcolm Brown is Director of Mission and Public Affairs for the Archbishops' Council of the Church of England. He has been a parish priest, an industrial chaplain and Principal of the Eastern Region Ministry Course. For ten years, he was Director of the William Temple Foundation in Manchester, specializing in Christian Ethics and Political Economy. He is the author of a number of books on ethics and social theology. He is an Honorary Lecturer at the University of Bath where he teaches on Ethics and Artificial Intelligence, and Visiting Professor in Theology at the University of Winchester.

Niamh Colbrook is a PhD candidate in Christian Theology at the University of Cambridge, where she also completed her BA and MPhil degrees in Theology. Her doctoral research focuses on theological approaches to suffering, materiality, and embodiment through the lens of eating disorders. She engages with disciplines such as psychology, psychiatry, anthropology and phenomenology, and works primarily in dialogue with the theology of Augustine of Hippo.

Shermara J. J. Fletcher is a millennial leader in the faith, homelessness and public life space. In her role as the Director of the William Seymour Project at the Centre of Theology and Community and Director of The Open Table at St George-in-the-East church, she equips Pentecostal churches and former homeless and housed people to act together for action and justice. As a MA graduate at St Mellitus College, she believes that the kingdom of God is found in what is considered 'the least of these' and is committed to developing this leadership to transform the churches' culture.

Tim Gorringe is Emeritus Professor of Theology at the University of Exeter. He has written two books and numerous articles on Theology and the Built Environment and has a particular interest in low-impact development.

Nicola Harris developed a particular passion for homes and community through volunteering at the launch of the Bristol Housing Festival in 2018 as her community placement for her ministerial training at Trinity College, Bristol. Through essays on this course, Nicola started to reflect on the housing crisis and the Church's response, taking the role of chaplain to the Bristol Housing Festival in 2019. Seeking to gain more experience in the housing sector following her two-year training at Trinity College, she is now working full time as a Project Support Worker and Chaplain for the Bristol Housing Festival. Nicola hopes to carry out her curacy alongside her Housing Chaplain role following her ordination in 2021. Nicola lives in Bristol with her husband, Matt, and their two girls, Elliana and Thea.

Mike Long is the minister at Notting Hill Methodist Church in West London, one of the most densely populated and unequal areas in Western Europe. The church stands close to the site of the Grenfell Tower fire of 2017 which claimed 72 lives. He chaired Shelter's Commission on Social Housing which published its report in 2019, and continues to campaign for more genuinely affordable housing and greater tenant empowerment. He also serves on the Faith and Order Committee of the Methodist Church.

Florence O'Taylor is a PhD researcher in the Department of Theology and Religion, Durham University, studying women's experiences of addiction through the lens of political theology. Previously, she led The Arch (www.arch76.co.uk), a Christian community that seeks to build relationship, and support women experiencing multiple forms of marginalization in the East End of London. She has also worked as a journalist and as a project worker at Charis (www.charislondon.org), a drug and alcohol rehabilitation centre for men at risk of homelessness in Whitechapel, London. She currently lives in Stanley, County Durham and, concurrently with her PhD, is exploring what radical, residential Christian community alongside women survivors of trauma could look like in this context.

Angus Ritchie is Director of the Centre for Theology and Community, and Assistant Priest at St George-in-the-East, Shadwell. He has served for over 20 years in east London parishes involved in community organizing, taking action on issues including affordable housing and homelessness. Angus is co-author of *Abide in Me: Catholic Social Thought and Action on Housing Challenges in England and Wales 2018–30* (London: Caritas Social Action Network, 2018). His latest book, *Inclusive Populism: Creating Citizens in the Global Age* was published in 2019 (Notre Dame, IN: University of Notre Dame Press).

Selina Stone is Tutor and Lecturer in Political Theology at St Mellitus College. Her PhD research at the University of Birmingham considers the embodied spirituality of Progressive Pentecostalism in the formation of political theology. Before joining St Mellitus, Selina worked as a community organizer and programme coordinator at the Centre for Theology and Community in East London. Her work focused on Pentecostal engagement in community organizing, the development of congregations for public action, and coordination of the Buxton Leadership Programme.

Jez Sweetland has initiated and managed strategic development in a variety of settings. He initially qualified as a lawyer and worked in London, and his previous positions include CEO of a barrister's chambers and CEO of a charitable national skills training organization. He founded the Bristol Housing Festival in 2018 and believes collaboration is the key to lasting social development. Jez lives in Bristol with his wife, Joanna, and his three children, Nathaniel, Evelina and Bethany.

Graham Tomlin is Bishop of Kensington and President of St Mellitus College. He taught theology at Oxford University, and was appointed the first Dean of St Mellitus College which is now one of the largest Anglican theological colleges in the world. He became Bishop of Kensington in 2015, was involved in the response to the Grenfell Tower fire in 2017, and is the Vice Chair of the Archbishop of Canterbury's Commission on Housing, Church and Community. He is the author of many books and articles, including *Looking through the Cross* (London: Bloomsbury – the Archbishop of Canterbury's Lent Book for 2014) and, most recently, *Bound to be Free: The Paradox of Freedom* (London: Bloomsbury, 2017).

Samuel Wells is an author, theologian and broadcaster. He is Vicar of St Martin-in-the-Fields in Trafalgar Square and Visiting Professor of Christian Ethics at King's College London. In 1998–2003 he was closely involved in the North Earlham, Larkman and Marlpit Development Trust, which arose from New Labour's New Deal for Communities regeneration programme. He is a trustee of The Connection at St Martin's, one of London's foremost homeless centres, and of St Martin's Charity, which distributes £4m a year to help people out of homelessness and whose Frontline Network links 1,500 homeless support workers across the UK.

Foreword

JUSTIN WELBY, THE ARCHBISHOP
OF CANTERBURY

Sometimes it takes a crisis to illuminate problems that have been in front of our noses for years. Writing now, after three months of Covid-19 lockdown, as the world faces a historically enormous economic downturn, it is becoming clearer that continuing to deepen old inequalities is unacceptable in a democracy. Unless we can resolve the old inequalities that have bequeathed us the crisis in housing, the chance seems remote of coming out of the Covid-19 crisis with much of our social fabric intact.

It is not as if the housing crisis was unforeseen. When I wrote about housing in *Reimagining Britain: Foundations for Hope* in 2018 (London: Bloomsbury Continuum), I was able to build on other distinguished studies and working groups which had analysed the problem and proposed ways to fix it. I added my voice to theirs for two reasons. The first was because the message has to be banged home remorselessly – the lack of decent and affordable housing for the people of this nation is a scandal that must be addressed with imagination and determination; across parties, across institutions and across communities.

My second reason explains why I am glad to see and commend this book. Although there have been many powerful analyses of the crisis in housing, driven by a profound commitment to a flourishing society, the Church's concern for good housing starts in a slightly different place. The common good is a central consequence of our teaching about and our discipleship for Jesus Christ. We draw from deep within the Christian tradition to understand the significance of good housing and good communities in a vision of God's kingdom.

Two strands of thought about how and where we live meet in the Scriptures. Jesus described himself as 'the Son of Man [who] has nowhere to lay his head', and human responses to God's call often mean leaving familiar and safe contexts to set out for the unknown. This is a kind of life that can be lived better from a tent than a mansion. But there is also the strand of theological insight that is committed to building lasting communities, even in an alien culture. Together, these theological themes teach us to commit to building deep relationships, with each other and with the places where we are set – and yet to live provisionally because the call to discipleship always lays us open to the unexpected.

So, because the Scriptures and Christian theology tell nuanced stories about housing and community, I was clear that, when I followed *Reimagining Britain* by setting up a Commission on Housing, Church and Community, the work should be driven by constant theological reflection. It is not enough that the Church gets involved in the messy business of building a better society, whether in times of crisis or of stability. Christians need to be clear about the source of their concern and their mandate for action – both, ultimately, to be found in the unswerving love of God and the revelation of God's will in Scripture.

This book begins to do some theological hard work about housing. It is also a book that brings theology into dialogue with practice – often deeply self-sacrificial practice, since responding to the housing crisis is not just about policies and economics, but about personal commitment to others.

There is a long way to go before Britain can be proud of the way its people are housed. I believe this book makes it abundantly clear why the state of our housing is very much central to the hope of the nation and very much the business of the Church.

++Justin Welby
Archbishop of Canterbury
July 2020

Preface

GRAHAM TOMLIN AND

MALCOLM BROWN

This book is one of the outcomes of the Archbishop of Canterbury's Commission on Housing, Church and Community. The Commission was set up in 2019 following Archbishop Justin Welby's book *Reimagining Britain*. In that book he explored a number of aspects of modern life and tried to spell out a vision of what transformation would look like in the light of the Christian gospel in a number of different fields. The Commission on Housing aimed to dig deeper into one of these themes, taking its starting point from Archbishop Justin's insight that we need to build communities and not just houses.

Both the editors of this book have been involved in the Commission from its earliest stages. Bishop Graham Tomlin became especially interested in housing after the Grenfell Tower fire of 2017 which happened in one of the parishes for which he is responsible as Bishop of Kensington. The fire revealed how neglect of housing safety, lack of adequate social housing and a willingness to allow the gap between rich and poor to grow to unhealthy levels was literally deadly. With this experience still fresh, Graham was invited to become Vice Chair of the Archbishop of Canterbury's Commission, and in particular to develop the theological framework for the work. Malcolm Brown, who is Director of the Mission and Public Affairs team for the Church of England, is a Christian ethicist with many years' experience of doing theology in the public sphere, including working in the 1990s with the William Temple Foundation to study church-related housing projects in Manchester. His role here was to get the Commission off the ground and to work with Graham on the theological content.

As we began the work of Commission, we were aware that we were treading in the footsteps of many before us. There are a large number of reports, commissions and proposals that have been produced over recent years to try to solve what is commonly called the housing crisis. What would make our report different? We were approaching this task explicitly as a Christian Commission, and particularly within the Church of England, and so the challenge was to think clearly about what a Christian approach to housing might look like. Might it be possible that the light shed by Jesus Christ, the light of the world, into the dark places of housing injustice and poverty could help us reimagine what good housing looks like and shine new light on a crisis that has defeated the best efforts of many governments and specialists over the years? Our hope was that a Christian view on housing would inform our further proposals to government, to the wider Church and dioceses and to the local church.

Yet, if we expected there to be an extensive literature on the theology of housing we were destined to be disappointed. Despite the fact that land, houses and dwelling places have always been a basic and universal human requirement, and indeed a constant theme throughout the Bible, there was remarkably little theological work on the specific question of housing available. A notable exception was Tim Gorringe's work on the built environment. We are delighted that he has contributed to this book. With a few other exceptions, it was hard to find many serious and sustained analyses of what a Christian approach to housing might look like. It seemed to us that we could attempt to fill something of that gap, or at least start a conversation. This book is the result. Some of the chapters in the book were initially papers delivered at a symposium on the theology of housing in Lambeth Palace in September 2019, and others have been commissioned since then.

Theology is never entirely divorced from practice and the book moves from more systematic or theologically driven approaches to housing towards some more practice-based and theologically informed approaches to certain aspects of housing policy. In some of these, it becomes clear how addressing a completely different set of issues takes one back, again and again, to the problems associated with housing: the lack of it and often its unsuitability.

The book deliberately combines contributions from established and well-known theologians and practitioners, and some younger emerging voices. It opens with Graham Tomlin asking how the Church bears witness to the gospel through housing. He maps a theology of housing on to the broad narrative of the Christian gospel which tells the story from Creation to New Creation, via the Fall, the incarnation and the birth of the Church. It results in five key factors for a Christian approach to housing: sustainability, security, stability, sociability and satisfaction. These five themes paint a picture of what housing policy should aspire to if it is to bear witness to the gospel of Christ. This is followed by a rich and provocative chapter by Tim Gorringe outlining a trinitarian shape for housing, issuing in six related and complementary themes of sustainability, justice, community, empowerment, beauty and the priority of life. Stephen Backhouse, one of the commissioners, follows with a stimulating meditation upon the call to be gentle space makers, building on the idea of *kenosis* in Philippians 2, and the priority of neighbourhood over nation, rooted in his study of Søren Kierkegaard. Malcolm Brown then explores the paradoxes of housing rooted in the ambiguity in Scripture about permanent settlement, issuing in the notion of the Church as resident aliens in the world and yet seeking the welfare of the city in which it is placed. Sam Wells goes on to draw on his own experience of involvement in community building to explore what redemption and regeneration might look like in housing policy, arguing that the Church needs to speak the language of hope and the vital importance of health, good work and relationships in building community life.

The book then proceeds to some more worked examples of what housing looks like when seen through the lens of Christian faith. Shermara Fletcher, Angus Ritchie and Selina

Stone offer a fascinating comparison of the complementary insights of the Catholic and Pentecostal traditions in relation to housing, involving the openness to the work of the Holy Spirit in stirring the Church to action and disrupting racial and power structures within the world that often issue in poor standard housing or unjust structures of social life. Niamh Colbrook explores the themes of materiality, suffering and flourishing and what it means to build with integrity, bearing in mind our embodied nature. Mike Long, who was one of the key Christian leaders in the North Kensington community at the time of the Grenfell Tower fire, tackles the issue of housing stigma, exploring what the concept of 'home' means and the impact of insecure housing while stressing the need for tenant voice and for more social housing. Florence O'Taylor then examines the effect of the housing crisis on a specific demographic – women with addictions – and the common link with homelessness, domestic violence and abuse. She develops a reimagined vision of housing based on the idea of friendship as a tool for liberation towards a more humane and stable form of housing. The book closes with a chapter by Nicola Harris and Jez Sweetland examining the theme of hospitality through some lived examples of what building community looks like in practice from personal experience rooted in their context in Bristol.

Our hope is that this is not the last word on housing. We hope that this book will provide stimulation for those Christians working in the housing industry, professional theologians interested in this vital aspect of modern life, and Christians committed to building better communities in their neighbourhoods. Practical Theology is both an academic discipline and a practice. It is where theology meets the Christian vocation to transform the world. The built environment transforms and is transformed, but not always competently or justly. We hope this book may be a precursor of further Practical Theological engagement with housing.

We also hope and believe that the book will be of value to others beyond the Church, open to learning from some new insights and possibilities for housing. We trust it will be the start of a longer conversation on what Christians should both think, and consequently do, about housing in the future. Theology at its best can inspire visions of the future that can make a radical difference in our world – for all, not just Christians. If we and our collaborators have helped inspire some new approaches to housing that begin to provide solutions to problems that often seem intractable, the book will have done its job.

Petertide 2020

I

Coming Home: A Theology of Housing and Community

GRAHAM TOMLIN

There is no shortage of agencies with suggestions on how to solve the housing crisis. Charities, think tanks, housing associations, experts in housing policy and academics all have their proposals to solve a predicament that manifests itself in unaffordable accommodation, a lack of social housing, poor-quality living conditions and the persistent scandal of homelessness. The Church, however, is not just another social agency offering its solutions. Its primary loyalty, as Augustine insisted, is to the City of God, not to the City of this World. Its purpose is focused within the two great calls of the Church – to worship the God of Jesus Christ in the power of the Spirit and to bear witness to that same God.

That does not mean, however, that the Church has no interest in the messy business of this world, such as the building, buying or renting of homes. In fact, it is precisely in such a context that the Church bears its witness. The Church never bears witness to Christ in a vacuum – it always does it in the specific contexts of particular times and places. Unlike many social issues, housing affects everyone, without exception. Each one of us has a home, whether it is an expensive mansion, a tiny flat, or anything in between. Because it is so universal and because our homes have such an influence on our well-being, housing has to be a primary arena of life in which the Church bears witness to Christ and his kingdom. If the gospel and the call to discipleship has a claim on the whole of human

1

life, then the Church needs to think deeply about housing. As Miroslav Volf puts it, the story of the gospel 'is an invitation to make our nested homes – family home, city-home, homeland, earth-home – reflect in some measure that coming home of God which completes creation'.

The primary question for the Church is therefore not the obvious one – how to solve the problems in our housing market – but how can the Church bear witness to the gospel of Jesus Christ in relation to the housing crisis? That is the crucial question this chapter seeks to answer.

Walter Brueggemann has argued that land and its use is one of the primary themes of the Bible.[1] We might go further and say that the homes and houses that are built on land are also one of the key themes that run through the narrative arc of biblical history and theology.

The Bible tells the story of a journey from a God-provided home, moving out into a hostile world, followed by the long history of redemption which leads back home again, but to one that looks different from the first. Like the Prodigal Son, who leaves home only to return to it later in a 'new normal', the story takes the human race from its home with God in Eden, through expulsion from that home, to the place of return, to a final picture of God making his home with us (Rev. 21.3).

Tim Gorringe reminds us that 'all building expresses an ideology'.[2] So, for example, the current market-driven approach to housing so often expresses the idea that a home is a place to exclude people, or a reward for success, or an asset to shield against the winds of change, something to put our trust, savings and wealth into. A Christian approach to housing is one that unashamedly embodies a vision of the story of the gospel. There are at least five pivotal 'moments' in this story: Creation, Fall, Redemption, the New Community and the New Creation. A theology of housing, church and community emerges from this story and takes shape as a witness to it in so far as it maps on to this story.

2

Creation, Sustainability and Stewardship

In the beginning, the original creation was pronounced 'good' (Gen. 1.31). It was given as a home for animal life of various kinds and, ultimately in time, the human race. The Garden of Eden is a picture of the divine provision of a space in which people can flourish and find fellowship with God, with other humans and with the rest of the created order.

Two central themes emerge in the Bible's view of created land. Chris Wright points out that these are held together in two key themes of the psalms: 'The earth is the LORD's and all that is in it' (Ps. 24.1), and 'the earth he has given to human beings' (Ps. 115.16).[3] The earth, or the land, is both God's property and God's gift.

The witness of the prophets and the writings is that, on the one hand, the specific Promised Land was never ultimately Israel's to own, as it remained God's possession, yet on the other hand it was given as a gift to Israel, as an inalienable expression and embodiment of God's generosity and love for his people. The gift of land was intended to bind the people to one another and to the God in whom they found their identity and wellbeing. Land, homes and houses were given not to create individual isolated enclaves, but to create a community in fellowship with God and one another.[4] With land comes moral obligation: land possession was dependent on observance of the Torah, otherwise the land will be lost. And that is of course exactly what happened in the exile.

To translate this into terms familiar with housing and property, God is (as it were) the freeholder of land, which is then 'leased' to humans as a gift. This of course radically relativizes human ownership of land. If God has all the rights and privileges of land ownership, then we are only ever the tenants and trustees of land. Moreover, with this gift of leased land, humanity is given responsibilities to 'work it and take care of it' (Gen. 2.15). Responsibility for proper care and preservation of land falls to the tenants. Land ownership brings with it not the licence to exact as much produce or revenue from it as it

3

will yield, but the responsibility to treat it well, and to ensure it is shared equitably.[5]

A housing policy that reflects the divine ownership and gifted nature of creation would therefore need to pay attention to the moral issues of the protection and sustainability of the land on which houses are built. Housing developments that are unsustainable, in the sense that they use too much of the earth's resources, are wasteful of energy or are out of sympathy with the natural environment, cannot bear witness to this part of the story.[6] We need to think of ourselves as stewards, not rulers of the natural world and of the properties we own or let out for rent. Housing policy needs to work with the grain of creation, to safeguard and not do violence to the earth God has given us.

Fallenness, Security and Justice

The second key moment in the biblical narrative is that of the Fall. The human race, the very part of creation singled out to bear the divine image, to protect, nurture and develop the creation, revolts against its maker and is consequently banished from the Garden that was intended as their home. From this point on, their experience is one of violence (the killing of Abel in chapter 4), of nature as an enemy rather than a friend (the flood in chapters 6—9), and of confusion (the Tower of Babel in chapter 11). The security and safety of Eden is exchanged for the insecurity of a cold and hostile world. Left to its own devices, land and housing become concentrated in the hands of a few and divisions grow between rich and poor.

In the early days of Hebrew possession of the land, it seems to have been allocated to tribes, and within that to families – generationally extended kinship groups that each possessed a portion of the land to sustain life and economic viability.[7] By the eighth century BC, a number of social changes – including a centralizing of state power, imposition of high levels of taxation, the growth of a wealthy class through the expansion of Solomon's empire, and battles with surrounding powers such as the Assyrians that decimated the peasantry – all led

4

to a concentration of land and property in fewer hands, and the loss of land from the family kinship groups that originally farmed it.

The result was not just poverty, injustice and division, but ultimately exile and land loss. As the prophet Isaiah put it:

Woe to you who add house to house
and join field to field
till no space is left
and you live alone in the land.

The LORD Almighty has declared in my hearing:

'Surely the great houses will become desolate,
the fine mansions left without occupants.'

Therefore my people will go into exile
for lack of understanding;
those of high rank will die of hunger
and the common people will be parched with thirst.
(Isa. 5.8–10, 13)

When land use gets out of kilter, all kinds of social problems begin to rear their heads, and a society cannot last long when land is misused. The Old Testament was no stranger to a housing crisis.

To deny people a share in the land and the sense of belonging that went with it was wrong, not because it infringed some modern principle of the sacredness of private property, but because being unable to share in the land meant being shut out from the community that enjoys together the grace and goodness of God. It meant denying people access to the life into which God had invited them – a life fully enjoying the blessing of God and neighbour, a full participation in the life God intended them to live. If the gift of God to people was land, then denying some people access to some form of trustee-ship of land was to sever their relationship to God as the Giver and to the covenant community that held that land.

As Israel entered the promised land, to ensure the ongoing possibility of people sharing in the blessing of that land, the enactment of justice became vital. In this context Leviticus 25 becomes crucial, with its strong link between land possession and observance of the law: 'Follow my decrees and be careful to obey my laws, and you will live safely in the land. Then the land will yield its fruit, and you will eat your fill and live there in safety' (Lev. 25.18–19). Every 50 years there was to be a 'Jubilee year' – a recalibration of ownership, with slaves being freed, and everyone returning to their ancestral lands. In between, land prices were to be related to the Jubilee principle, with prices dropping the nearer it came to the deadline year. There is proper scholarly debate as to whether the Jubilee year, as described in this passage, was ever enacted, but either way it does indicate an ideal to which Israel aspired.

The basic principle of the Jubilee was not to prohibit land ownership or sale, or to impose absolute equality, but to protect land tenure by families so they were not allowed to drop out of the community into generational bondage. Those who ran up debts they could not pay would often have to sell land or even themselves into slavery. The Jubilee was a way to check that spiralling process into entrenched poverty. It also was designed to stop land being concentrated in a very few hands, as had happened in some of the surrounding nations where the kings owned all the land, with citizens as merely tenants and, as Isaiah 5 indicates, had begun to happen in Israel. The redemption of land, as Wright argues, 'was not provided so that an Israelite who, for whatever reason, failed to maintain his property should automatically and immediately have it restored to him, but that a person's descendants should not have to suffer in perpetuity the consequence of the economic collapse of his generation'.[8]

If this expresses the inner logic of a biblical view of land, as God's possession, yet gifted in trust to us, to create a communal life in fellowship with God and one another, then it suggests a challenge to a view that allows a spiral of land value taking it out of the range of many and only accessible to the economically fortunate.

The doctrine of the Fall narrates how this good world has been damaged, broken through the rejection of the Creator by the creation, and is thus vulnerable and liable to decay. Unaided, it will descend into social and environmental disintegration. Home is an expression of ourselves, in that we choose the colours, décor, hang pictures and personalize the space. The destruction of home, such as what happened at Grenfell Tower, is therefore a kind of desecration, an invasion of the self that is much more significant than the loss of an office block, or a railway station. As Marwa al-Sabouni put it: 'Our homes don't just contain our life earnings, they stand for what we are. To destroy one's home should be taken as an equal crime to destroying one's soul.'[9]

Housing that would bear witness to this part of the story of the gospel has, therefore, to pay attention to the need for security against the threats to shared land and proper housing. Home is intended to be a place where danger is kept at bay, a place of privacy where we know our own space will not be invaded against our will, and where we can feel secure from intrusion. Housing that testifies to the gospel needs to be safe space, offering shelter and security against damage and destruction, with proper regulation against the insecurity of unstable residence. It needs to provide security against volatile market forces that create insecure owning or renting scenarios that lead to precarious lives. It needs to enable both financial affordability and personal security for both home owners and those who rent.

This will, from time to time, as in the Jubilee principle, require specific intervention to prevent the (un)natural course of events whereby safe and secure housing is just the privilege of a few. Making housing secure requires attention to issues of justice. The sight of people living in insecure tenancies or temporary accommodation, vulnerable to rent rises at the whim of landlords or developers, or to eviction at short notice, precisely reflects the insecurity reflected in the biblical story of the Fall. Similarly, the way in which land continues to accrue more and more value over time, independent of any work done on it, so that landowners become increasingly wealthy while the houses on that land become unaffordable to anyone else, is a reflection not of the divine will for land to bind people together, but of the brokenness of God's world.

On the political left there is an ideal of the perfectibility of people. On the political right there is an ideal of the perfectibility of markets. Christians are sceptical of both in this life. The market is not the enemy, but neither is it the sole solution. Here we find a mandate for specific intervention to ensure that with regard to housing, markets reflect the vision of the kingdom of God – not the economic processes of a fallen world.

Redemption, Stability and Formation

The work of redemption of this broken world begins with the call of Abraham and the call of the people of Israel to the gift of living in a specific land provided by God. Christian faith later announces that into this broken world God has sent his Son, 'incarnate of the Virgin Mary', dying for the sins of the world, rising again for the redemption of all things, with the promise of the Holy Spirit who forms and perfects us and all creation into maturity.

This part of the gospel story speaks of God entering the human story of soil and flesh. Far from some deist God who creates the world and then leaves it to run its course, God gets his hands dirty in the dust of the earth, as it were, by calling a 'wandering Aramaean', by sending the prophets, and supremely in sending his Son, taking flesh, taking up residence in space and time. In Jesus Christ, 'the Word became flesh and blood, and moved into the neighbourhood' (John 1.14). God puts down roots in human flesh, history and places.

To bear witness to this part of the story, housing needs to provide the kind of stability that enables people to be rooted, or incarnate if you like, in places, staying in that same place for as long as they choose. Because of the incarnation, place and space matter. Stability means being able to put down roots, to feel we belong in a place and to a community over a period of time. Simone Weil, the French philosopher, wrote: 'To be rooted is perhaps the most important and least recognised need of the human soul.'[10] When one of the Grenfell Tower survivors was asked why the hotel room in which he was placed after the fire did not feel like home, his reply was simple: 'because it is not permanent'.

Part of sharing in the divine blessing, the invitation to life in fellowship with God, is the knowledge that we belong both to God and to a wider community. Being constantly uprooted from home denies us the capacity to belong, to develop long-term relationships that can bring support during difficult times and that help mould us into mature human beings. Stability in a physical place and community that enables us to put down roots is essential for the kind of formation to maturity that is crucial for human flourishing.

At the most basic level, we build houses for shelter. We need a place that can protect us from the elements of rain, sun or wind. Yet there is much more to a home than this. Wendell Berry asks the provocative question: What are People For?[11] The Christian answer to that, taking our cue from Jesus when asked almost the same question, must be that we are here to love God and to love our neighbour.

And yet that is not something that comes naturally to us. It might come naturally to love ourselves, but not necessarily to love our neighbour as ourselves. We have to learn it. And home is one of the key places that we learn to do this. Homes are places where we grow towards maturity, towards the goal of our earthly journey, which is to be with the God who is both our origin and our goal.

Humans are made to grow to maturity, which in Christian understanding means growth in love for God (which involves *gratitude* for all we have been given) and neighbour (which means *generosity* towards those placed right next to us). This is what mature humanity looks like. We therefore need contexts in which such formation happens. The primary place in which such formation happens, at least in our early years, is family, and there is a particularly strong link between family, home and housing in the Bible, particularly in the Hebrew Scriptures.

The book of Deuteronomy invites the people of God to study

the laws of God, and in particular to 'impress them on your children. Talk about them when you sit at home and when you walk along the road, when you lie down and when you get up' (Deut. 6.7; see also 11.10). The brief glimpses we get of Jesus as a child at home refer to his growth in maturity: '. . . they returned to Galilee, to their own town of Nazareth. And the child grew and became strong; he was filled with wisdom, and the grace of God was on him' (Luke 2.39–40). Elsewhere in the New Testament, the family home is presented as a place of formation and growth – which is the first commandment with a promise – 'so that it may go well with you and that you may enjoy long life on the earth . . . Fathers, do not exasperate your children; instead, bring them up in the training and instruction of the Lord' (Eph. 6.1–4).

In the earliest period of the Church, homes were routinely used as the venue for church life (e.g. 1 Cor. 16.19; Col. 4.15; Philem. 2). Home was a place for worship and communal life, alongside more formal settings for gathering: 'Every day they continued to meet together in the temple courts. They broke bread in their homes and ate together with glad and sincere hearts' (Acts 2.46). Home was a place of instruction, or formation, where in the context of family and wider friendships and relationships, both children and adults learnt wisdom and grew into maturity, bearing in mind that households in biblical times were much wider and more extensive than the nuclear family of today.

Homes and houses are one of the primary contexts in which we grow into maturity. This is particularly true for children but it is true for adults as well. Those who live together are necessarily shaped by the experience of having to live alongside and manage the joys and tensions of close proximity with others. Even those who live alone can and do find home a place of formation, through such regular practices as reading, watching TV or video, reflecting on life experiences, or welcoming others into their homes.

That is why we need stable housing – so we can put down roots in a place and a community and be formed by that community into maturity.

Community, Sociability and Generosity

The fourth 'moment' in the arc of the biblical narrative comes with Pentecost – the sending of the Spirit and the forming of a new community, the Church.

At the heart of the Christian gospel is welcome into fellowship, to communion with God, and with the people that he gathers. In creation we are provided with and welcomed into a world that is not ours, and we are urged to delight in it. Throughout the Hebrew Scriptures, the invitation of God is issued to his people to sit and eat with him:

> Everyone who thirsts,
> come to the waters;
> and you that have no money,
> come, buy and eat!
> Come, buy wine and milk
> without money and without price. (Isa. 55.1)

In the Eucharist, the invitation to sit and eat at the table of God is given physical form. The vision of the new Jerusalem concludes with the same invitation: 'The Spirit and the bride say, "Come." And let everyone who hears say, "Come." And let everyone who is thirsty come. Let anyone who wishes take the water of life as a gift' (Rev. 22.17).

Hospitality creates sociability. It is something we receive. It is also something we are called to give. David Walker, the Bishop of Manchester, tells the story of an immigrant to the UK who had been conscious of being a guest of his adopted nation for many years. On moving into his own home for the first time he remarked on how, on the first occasion, this enabled him to be host, not just guest, in a place that was now his own.[12] To be in a position to offer hospitality confers dignity on a person as imitating God in his own generosity.

The New Testament Greek word for 'hospitality' is *Philoxenia* – literally, 'love of the stranger' – and the theme is prominent in the list of characteristics that mark out a Christian view of home. Instructions to exhibit hospitality abound; for example:

- Contribute to the needs of the saints; extend hospitality to strangers (Rom. 12.13).
- Be hospitable to one another without complaining (1 Pet. 4.9).
- Do not neglect to show hospitality to strangers, for by doing that some have entertained angels without knowing it (Heb. 13.2).

The size and role of households has, of course, changed significantly since New Testament times. Most households are now smaller and the hospitality industry is much more developed. Now, when staying in an unfamiliar town, we use hotels and restaurants rather than rely on being taken into a local home. Showing hospitality to visitors is less of a cultural expectation than it was in biblical times.[13] Yet the practice remains, perhaps in a different shape, but as a central aspect of the way a home is to be used in Christian understanding, because hospitality creates community, and living in community is part of the divine will for human life.

Public space needs to be sociable, to create a sense of society. And to do this it needs to be generous. Marwa al-Sabouni, in her evocative description of the architecture of her home city of Homs, later destroyed in the Syrian conflict, speaks about older Syrian cities as 'generous cities' that offered free water fountains, benches and shady trees in open spaces during hot days. Public space was attractive and given priority in the design of housing development.[14] Housing that reflects God's welcome to us needs to provide space for hospitality and welcome. Overcrowded accommodation makes welcoming the neighbour or stranger difficult. Similarly, housing designed to build miniature castles, isolated enclaves that essentially shut out the neighbour and are incapable of building community, cannot bear witness to the gospel of welcome.

A home is not neutral community space. There is a need for such communal space in neighbourhoods. Yet homes and houses are also private spaces into which friends, neighbours and even strangers can be invited on occasion and when chosen by the host. If we are shaped and formed by interaction with others, then inviting them into our own personal and private space will be one way in which we allow ourselves to be formed by other people and invite them to be formed by us. It will also create a broader sense of community and welcome within a particular neighbourhood once this becomes normal practice. A Christian view of housing must include the possibility for anyone to act as host in their own home, however small or limited that may be.

Resurrection, Satisfaction and Technology

The culmination of the story of Jesus is his resurrection. The climax of the Bible is the resurrection of the world into a new creation, a vision of the earth restored, purged of suffering, misery and injustice, of the triumph of life and love. The vision of Revelation 21, with a city of jewels, with streets of gold and vibrant colour, is meant to evoke a sense of wonder at the beauty of this vision: 'It shone with the glory of God, and its brilliance was like that of a very precious jewel, like a jasper, clear as crystal' (Rev. 21.11). This is no grey, colourless place, a brutalist concrete prison, but a city that shines with splendour. It is a place of streets, buildings, walls, gates and measuring sticks. In other words, it is a place where human artifice, ingenuity and technology is used not to deny life or to dull the senses, but to create beauty, to allow in the light of God's glory, to create a space for human and other life to find joy.

People flourish and mature well in spaces that they enjoy and which stimulate wonder and pleasure. Dull, harsh and unforgiving built environments do not encourage investment in those places, nor the communities they contain – a brutal environment brutalizes people. To take pleasure in our environment is to take pride in it, to want to preserve and make it stable, to ensure its sustainability and longevity. Tim Gorringe writes about an 'aesthetics of creation, responding sympathetically to the environment, rather than trying to "tame" it'.[15]

The beauty of the new Jerusalem is tied up with what lies at its centre: the fact that God dwells with mortals. It is lit not by the sun, but by the glory of God. What makes the city beautiful is not just its stones, but its relationships. Hence Gorringe also writes of the 'aesthetics of community', and points to the conditions that can make the built environment beautiful – namely, respect for the natural created environment; exuding life; respect for the past; communal spaces and buildings; caring for the poor and their living conditions.[16]

Housing needs to give a deep sense of satisfaction. Our homes need not just to be functional spaces, but places we enjoy living in, we delight to come home to, just as we long to come home to our true destination in the new Jerusalem. Attention to the aesthetic quality of accommodation will be important for a Christian vision of housing that can be a sign of the new creation. It will also be significant for the aspect of home as a place of formation. The beauty or otherwise of the built environment has a significant impact on mental health and hence wellbeing.[17] We shrink in places of drabness, but flourish and are able to grow in places of beauty and life.

Conclusion

How can the Church bear witness to the gospel of Christ in the arena of housing? The Church of England in particular is both a major landowner and also has a voice in public policy through its established status in society. The Church can bear its witness to the gospel by building houses and housing developments that explicitly seek to display the elements we have seen emerging from the narrative arc of Scripture: housing that is sustainable, secure, stable, sociable and satisfying. Although this is a Christian vision for housing, it is also one that hopefully others outside the Church can recognize and own. The Church can also therefore argue for such values to permeate public housing policy, in such a way that we see ourselves as stewards rather than controllers of the earth, alert to the call of justice, seeking spaces for human formation into maturity, exhibiting a generosity of space and place, and housing that brings delight and joy, because that is what we were made for.

Notes

1 Brueggemann, W. (2002), *The Land: Place as Promise and Challenge in Biblical Faith*, Minneapolis, MN: Fortress Press.

2 Gorringe, T. J. (2002), *A Theology of the Built Environment: Justice, Empowerment, Redemption*, Cambridge: Cambridge University Press, pp. 26–36.

3 Wright, C. J. H. (1990), *God's People in God's Land: Family, Land and Property in the Old Testament*, Carlisle: Paternoster, p. 116.

4 Wright, *God's People*, pp. 135ff.

5 For expansion of this point, see Brueggemann, *The Land*, pp. 56–62.

6 This point is made strongly in Gorringe, *A Theology of the Built Environment*, ch. 9.

7 See Wright, *God's People*, ch. 2.

8 Wright, *God's People*, p. 124.

9 al-Sabouni, M. (2016), *The Battle for Home*, London: Thames & Hudson, p. 57.

10 Weil, S. (2002), *The Need for Roots*, London: Routledge, p. 43.

11 Berry, W. (1990), *What Are People For? Essays by Wendell Berry*, New York: North Point Press.

12 Francis, A. (2016), *Foxes Have Holes: Christian Reflections on Britain's Housing Need*, London: Ekklesia, p. 9.

13 See Pohl, C. (1999), *Making Room: Recovering Hospitality as a Christian Tradition*, Grand Rapids, MI: Eerdmans. For an excellent discussion of the significance of hospitality in Christian history and activity, Richard Sennett remarks on the shift in the nineteenth century from public space in cities as a place where you would expect to meet and interact with strangers, to one where you would expect to be left alone: Sennett, R. (2018), *Building and Dwelling: Ethics for the City*, London: Allen Lane, pp. 27f.

14 al-Sabouni, *The Battle for Home*, ch. 3.

15 Gorringe, *A Theology*, p. 208.

16 Gorringe, *A Theology*, pp. 217–20.

17 See Heaven, W. (2019), 'What Building Beautiful Can Do for Mental Health', in Airey, J., *Building More, Building Beautiful: How Design and Style Can Unlock the Housing Crisis*, London: Policy Exchange, pp. 112–17.

Theological Priorities for Housing

TIM GORRINGE

Why Theology?

You may often read that Christianity is hostile to concern with
the built environment, or to the very idea of 'home'. Although
the writers of such work have clearly never read Jeremiah 29,
they can appeal to the fact that the built environment has never
constituted a locus in Christian ethics or aesthetics, as standard textbooks show. Behind this neglect lies two millennia of
Platonizing reflection which makes a sharp distinction between
body and soul, earthly and heavenly, spiritual and material.
This distinction can be understood as a rationalization of
both the brevity of life and the appalling housing most human
beings have had to endure and still endure. A moment's reflection, however, shows that concern with the built environment
is implicit in the very foundations of Christian faith. First there
is the Calvinist insistence, reprised critically in the Barmen
declaration of 1934, that God is the Lord of all life and that
therefore there is nothing outside divine concern. 'The earth is
the LORD's and all that is in it' (Ps. 24.1) – the hermeneutical
key to Jesus' response to the question about tribute to Caesar
(Mark 12.13–17). To be human is to be placed: to be born in
this house, hospital, stable (according to Luke); to live in this
slum, shanty, council house, semi-detached, tower block, farmhouse, mansion; to go to school through these streets or lanes;
to play in this alley, park, garden; to shop in this market, that
mall; to work in this factory, mine, office, farm.[1] The NAME
– the origin and end of all things – in Jesus entered into this

world, knew what we call the built environment at first hand. Many of the encounters in the Gospels happen in a house. John of Damascus, reflecting on this, summed up its significance in the lapidary definition that 'matter matters'. Equally, Paul's blinding vision on the Damascus road taught him that if Jesus is the brother of every human being then all are equal in him (Gal. 3.28). But this belief has consequences for the built environment. How is it possible to believe that the rich man lives in his castle and the poor man at his gate if that be true? This conviction was the passion behind the concern of the nineteenth-century Christian socialists with slum clearance and providing decent housing for 'the poor'. It has huge implications for the way in which we build – and indeed structure – society.

Marx remarked that the difference between the worst of architects and the best of bees was that the architect raised the structure in his or her imagination first. But what is imagination? According to our Scriptures it is God's Spirit that is the source of all generous visions, all dreams of the world that we pray for in the Lord's prayer ('May your kingly rule be realized'). We know from the letters of Paul that an intense experience of what he spoke of as God's Spirit characterized the first Christian generation, changing the way in which they prayed and viewed the world. Luke distils this in the story of Pentecost which cites Joel 2 as the key to what is going on (Acts 2.17; Joel 2.28). Now, we know that there are not only generous dreams but also nightmares, and many of these nightmares took flesh in twentieth-century building. We have to discern the spirits, whether they are of God (1 John 4.1). But dreams and visions that lead to fullness of life derive from God the Spirit and they seek concrete realization, among other things, in the forms of shelter we build, in our schools, hospitals and public buildings.

Drawing on Plato's appropriation of Pythagoras Vitruvius, in the first century BC, in a work that inspired the Renaissance, argued that the human being is to the universe as microcosm is to macrocosm, and the proportions of the human body are determinative for architecture. Building, that is to say, presupposes an anthropology, but all theology is anthropology, in the sense that our understanding of the origin and end of all things, God or the NAME, determines what we believe about the human. Christian anthropology, therefore, has something to say about how we build. As in every other area of Christian ethics there is a debate without consensus: the Jesuit Villapanda, at the end of the sixteenth century, and John Wood the elder, the designer of the Royal Crescent at Bath, both believed that God had revealed that we had to build using the classical orders; Abbot Suger, the architect of Chartres, and Pugin in the nineteenth century, believed that Gothic was the only proper Christian architecture. As in every area of Christian reflection we take our place and, arguing from our Scriptures, and with reference to our predecessors, argue our own position.

Christian concern with the built environment has a Trinitarian shape, as seen in the box below.

	GOD THE CREATOR	GOD THE RECONCILER	GOD THE REDEEMER
Known in	Order	Embodiment	Creativity
Built environment Correlate	Planning	Structuring community	Utopian vision
Theological/ ethical Reflection	Values that underlie planning	Priority of life together 'breaking barriers': Race – ghettoes	Nature of the human home
Realization	Common good Human scale	Class – social housing Gender – patriarchal space	Gracious building and planning
		Place	
Core concept	Ecology		Empowerment

The goal of all our building is what the Deuteronomists called 'rest', *shalom*, the realization of God's will for humankind. In a smallholder society they envisaged every family under its vine and fig tree. Our task in the twenty-first century is to work out what this means for nine billion or more people. Towards that end I will, in the remainder of this chapter, outline six theological priorities for the building of houses.

The Priority of Sustainability

I take it for granted that the threats that natural scientists have been calling our attention to for the past 40 years – resource depletion, loss of biodiversity, climate change, all related to a burgeoning world population – have to be taken with the utmost seriousness. This is especially incumbent on Christians given their understanding of all created reality as gift, an ecstatic expression of God's love so that abusing, trashing or destroying creation is not just bad stewardship but, as Wendell Berry puts it, 'the most horrid blasphemy'. There are, of course, those who dispute the science, but I will not argue the case here. In the context of this discussion it is important to recognize the impact of the built environment. When it comes to global warming, for example, Allan Rodger describes the built environment as 'the principal villain' in the story.[2] In Britain the use of buildings accounts for 46 per cent of carbon dioxide emissions and when construction is added it is more than 50 per cent. Energy is consumed in vast quantities at every stage of the process – in the production of bricks, cement, steel, aluminium, glass, plaster; in their transport and assembly, and then heating, cooling and lighting buildings once they have been built. The construction industry uses an estimated 3 billion tonnes of raw materials per year – 40 per cent of the total flow into the global economy. The OECD nations consume half the world's commercial energy and 40 per cent of this comes from heating, lighting and providing air conditioning for homes and offices.[3] Some of this demand is generated by building that is insensitive to local conditions. Notoriously, Le Corbusier wanted 'one single building for all nations and climates'. Ignoring local climates means installing huge heating and air conditioning systems in offices, factories, homes and hotels around the world.[4] The Sears tower in Chicago uses more energy in 24 hours than an average American city of 150,000 or an Indian city of more than 1 million.[5] New York City uses as much electrical energy as the whole continent of Africa.

One of the things that follows from this is that in order to be sustainable it is not sufficient simply to fit all buildings with solar panels or ground source heat pumps, though both may be desirable. More fundamentally we have to ask what vision of society we want our buildings to embody, and what materials we ought to use. The question 'How should we build?' implies a vision of society as a whole. Human ecology is part of planetary ecology. This means that questions about building cannot be divorced from questions of culture, politics and spirituality. At the moment, in England, most building follows a suburban vision, resting on an individualist anthropology, and tailored to the needs of the affluent. This account is simply not sustainable. We all know that for the whole world to look like the United States we need five planets, and to look like Europe three planets – but we only have one. To take that seriously involves changing our understanding of the good society and the good life, both in relation to settlements and to houses. A now forgotten document, Local Agenda 21, laid out as its goals, among other things, that in order to have a viable future it was necessary to

- promote development that reduces the need to travel;
- encourage a shift away from car use towards less environmentally damaging modes of travel;
- encourage energy-efficient and environmentally benign building practices;
- tackle fuel poverty through improving the energy efficiency of low-income housing;
- encourage resource and energy-efficient patterns of development;
- constrain development within natural carrying capacity limits.

Simon Fairlie remarks that if planning authorities would make it relatively easy to obtain planning permission for low-impact sustainable buildings, and correspondingly difficult to obtain permission for high-impact unsustainable ones, it would go a long way towards meeting these environmental obligations.[6] Building sustainably, then, means, in the first place, understanding the need for low-impact building.

Low-impact buildings are usually, though not always, found in the countryside. They use local and traditional materials like wood, cob and straw bales, and usually make use of recycled materials. They are self-built and cost very little (which is to say, they are genuinely affordable, which is true of very little housing in Britain at this time). At present, planning authorities routinely give permission for high-impact unsustainable developments and equally routinely oppose low-impact development. In 2018 a community of 21 people, men, women and children, who had lived in a low-impact community for 18 years just outside Moretonhampstead, in Devon, were evicted and their dwellings destroyed. The site, in the middle of a wood, was more or less invisible; it was off grid; used compost toilets; and only the water was provided by what today we call 'utilities'. The adult members of the community all worked in the area and contributed to the local economy. If one asks the reason for what one observer called the 'bone headed nastiness' of this action the principal one appears to be that such developments do not fit into an upper-middle-class view of society. Not a Range Rover or electric gate in sight. This clearly alarmed both the wealthy neighbours of the Steward Community Woodland, and also the planners. Fairlie notes that traditional building styles developed by finding inspired solutions to problems that arose through access to only a limited range of materials. He comments: 'If we are to rediscover an architecture that is dynamic yet remains authentically traditional, we can only do so by giving builders free rein to solve functional problems with the similarly limited, but updated, range of basic local materials. And if such an architecture is to flourish, the obvious arena is that of low-impact development.'[7]

Second, a lesson from 1943. In 1941 Plymouth was bombed flat, and the Professor of Town Planning at the University of London, Patrick Abercrombie, was appointed to draw up the plan for its rebuilding. The plan is an object lesson in dreaming

dreams and having visions. Abercrombie was writing at the
height of the U-boat Campaign, when Great Britain was almost
starved into surrender. Accordingly, fundamental to his plan
was a grading of Plymouth's land from 1 to 6, with 1 as the best
and 6 the worst. Abercrombie noted that we would never build
on grade 1 land as that would be 'blasphemy'. Fast forward 70
years and the city of Exeter has been building on grade 1 agricultural land, literally as if there were no tomorrow. I pointed
this out to the local MP, and he replied: 'People have to live
somewhere.' But according to the Food and Agriculture Organization, topsoil, on which the world relies for its food, and that
takes 1,000 years to form, is diminishing year on year even
as world population grows year on year. Furthermore, climate
change means that each year more and more land is taken out
of production, a process exacerbated by urbanization. Karl
Barth argued that stupidity was one of the fundamental forms
of sin and I submit that not to heed Abercrombie's rule, to
build anywhere on grade 1 land, is a primary exemplification
of stupidity as sin, which our councils, developers and politicians are committing day by day without a breath of protest.
Kevin Anderson, of the Tyndall Centre in Manchester, believes
that holding global warming to 2°C is impossible and we may
rise to 4°C. If that happens the world our grandchildren live
in will be one of unimaginable famine because such a temper-
ature rise will take out 40 per cent of the world's staple crops.
Therefore, for God's sake (not an oath but a theological principle), let us never build on grade 1 agricultural land.

The Priority of Justice

Do we need reminding that some of the most incisive words
about justice in our Scriptures concern housing, and specifically second homes (Amos 3.15, 5.11; Isa. 3.14–15, 5.7ff.; Jer.
22.13ff.)? The dimensions of such justice are manifold: they
include the way in which huge areas of Great Britain (Devon,
(especially Exmoor), Cornwall, and other 'desirable' areas)
are socially destroyed by second home ownership, hollowing

out community, closing schools and making homes for local people unaffordable. This phenomenon in turn follows from the growing inequality throughout the world, where the top 1 per cent or 5 per cent or 10 per cent earn more than the whole of the rest of the population put together (as documented by Thomas Piketty in *Capital in the Twenty First Century*).

The demands of justice include opposing the way in which houses have become a key area for financial investment. When council house stock was sold off in the 1980s many people with spare cash bought these houses to rent, as rents give far better returns than the stock market. 'Buy to let' advertisements can be found on the pages of many estate agents. Since the financial crash of 2008 global investment firms have taken this opportunity 'bigtime' so that finance capital now owns huge parts of London, Berlin and cities all around the world, as documented in Fredrik Gertten's film *Push*. According to the 1948 Declaration of Human Rights, housing is a right, and not a market opportunity. Much of what we call the housing crisis stems from this practice, which consists in buying up low-cost housing, giving it a makeover, and selling it off again – or preferably renting it – for prices the poor cannot afford. We know what Amos or Isaiah would have said about this. We need legislation to make sure that housing is not simply a market opportunity for the very rich.

At the same time Leviticus reminds us repeatedly to care for the *ger*, the foreign worker, and Deuteronomy insists on remembering that we were once refugees, and should care for them. So justice cannot forget the boat people, the tens of thousands crowded into refugee camps on the fringes of Europe, threatening the livelihoods of the people living there, but desperate for somewhere safe to live. Within our own country the traveller community, which has mobile homes, is the object of frequent vigilante attacks which include death threats and grievous bodily harm, and is currently threatened with criminalization by government legislation. As with low-impact housing this is about response to a group who do not fit into affluent middle-class norms.

And justice is not just about the present. Already in 1880

Ruskin reminded us that it has a future dimension, explicitly in relation to the built environment. 'God has lent us the earth for our life', he wrote. 'It is a great entail. It belongs as much to those who are to come after us . . . as to us; we have no right, by anything that we do or neglect, to involve them in unnecessary penalties, or deprive them of benefits that it was in our power to bequeath.'[8] So building and living sustainably is actually a matter of justice.

The Priority of Community

Christian anthropology understands human beings as made for relationship, formed by the God who is relationship in Godself, and therefore not fully human outside community. Because human beings are needy they have, for most of their history, lived in community, whether as hunter gatherers, or in the *polis* (a community of up to half a million), and until 30 years ago most humans who have ever lived, dwelt in a village, which Lewis Mumford believed was the cradle of ethics. Since the nineteenth century, however, there has been a rush to the city, in which more than half of humankind now live, and in response, at the same time, a search for escape from the crowd, a detached or semi-detached existence. This has led, in North America and the UK, to the creation of vast suburbs, covering millions of acres of fertile land in the quest for – what? A home of one's own? Autonomy? A patch of garden to cultivate? These things are not, in themselves, to be despised, but the question is what we should prioritize when we come to build. The garden city of Ebenezer Howard, the planning of early twentieth-century figures like Raymond Unwin and Patrick Abercrombie, all prioritized community. In the background of their work was Thomas More's *Utopia*, which describes a city of cooperatives, each consisting of 30 families who share common facilities and meals and who organize child care and other practical functions. Unwin had this in mind in Hampstead Garden City. He wanted communal kitchens, but the residents said no. Co-housing developments in Denmark in the 1990s had greater success. The architect Jan Gudmand-Hoyer commented, 'This will be the first city in the world where Thomas More's idea of Utopia is realized some five hundred years after it was conceived.'[9]

Co-housing, which is making ground in the United Kingdom at present, is building for community. A review of co-housing projects found that nearly every community wanted a larger common house to provide extra guest rooms, or rooms that can be rented out to teenage children or to a couple having relationship difficulties, or to people needing more work space. In Copenhagen there are 48 resident-managed co-housing communities. The first phase, completed in 1990, included 11 co-housing communities of 20–40 dwellings (300 units). Of these 11, 6 are non-profit owned rentals, 3 are cooperatively financed, and 3 are privately financed. Three of the communities are designed around covered streets. People car share and jointly own leisure items like boats. The idea is to have the family as a base but open it up to community. It turns out that such co-housing plays a strong role in local community with members active in the local theatre, politics, schools and sports teams.

Community, we know, is grounded in common work. Colin Ward documents the growth of a genuine spirit of community within a self-build project in Lewisham. A member of the group said:

> The one thing that's left me intensely proud is the cooperative spirit on the Brockley site. A wife had a baby the other week. The buntings were out and the balloons . . . If someone requires a babysitter . . . if someone's working on a car . . . or the communal garden . . . they get help. They pay a pound a week to a communal fund. They've landscaped the gardens last year. No one tells them to do that. They do it themselves because they have control over where they are living and they contribute.[10]

Housing cooperatives also allow people unable to afford to buy their own homes to have direct control over the provision of their own housing while at the same time receiving public sub-sidies.[11] Helping with the building process is usually involved and good for raising morale and for getting people working together. It, too, has social consequences. What is involved is 'Decentralization rather than centralization; self-help rather than dependency; participatory democracy rather than repre-sentative democracy; networking rather than hierarchy; setting long term objectives rather than short term.'[12] In other words, building sustainably involves a different vision of society to the present individualist paradigm. Christians should be open to this because at the heart of Scripture is a vision of a world made otherwise.[13]

The Priority of Empowerment

Commentaries on Acts do not always remind their readers that the story in Numbers 11 stands behind Joel 2, and therefore the story of Pentecost. Numbers, we suppose (following Ton Veer-kamp), derives from the period after the return from exile when feuding groups struggle for the vision of what really constitutes Israel (a bit like post-Brexit Britain). Should the Great Leader ('Moses') decide? The delightfully humorous and ironical story in Numbers 11 says no. First of all, power is delegated to 70 'elders', who all undergo a training programme, but when others who have not got their certificate join in 'Moses' says, 'Would that all the Lord's people were prophets!' – that is to say, would that all people shared in the tasks of fashioning community according to God's will. The Pentecost story says that that time has now arrived (Acts 2.16). Sadly, as we know, things quickly reverted to rulers and ruled, clergy and laity, those who knew and the ignoramuses.

Learning from this story is essential if we are to build homes successfully. Christopher Alexander writes that to build beauti-ful places, 'It is essential that the people of a society, together, *all the millions of them*, not just professional architects, design all the millions of places. There is no other way that human variety, and the reality of specific human lives, can find their way into the structure of places.'[14] You can see that this is Numbers 11 translated for the built environment. What Alexander wants to avoid is the tyranny of the expert: 'As soon as a few people begin to build for "the many", their patterns about what is needed become abstract; no matter how well meaning they are, their ideas gradually get out of touch with reality, because they are not faced with the living examples of what the patterns say.'[15] I shall write more below about the patterns Alexander mentions here.

The English architect John Turner, an enthusiast for the work of Patrick Geddes, worked in the Peruvian slums between 1957 and 1965. At that time slums were built on marginal land that had not been claimed. He argued that the way to deal with them was not to go for expensive schemes of state housing, but to support people in building for themselves. Housing, he said, was a verb. 'Questions about the consequences of housing in people's lives can only be asked in words that describe processes and relationships.'[16] He wanted to get away from the obsession with the number of housing units and insisted that the key question was what housing does in people's lives. 'When dwellers control the major decisions and are free to make their own contributions to the design, construction and management of their own housing', he and his fellow contributors wrote, 'both the process and the environment produced stimulate individual and social wellbeing. When people have no control or responsibility for key decisions in the housing process dwelling environments may instead become a barrier to personal fulfilment and a burden on the economy.'[17] He argued that only people and local organizations could provide the necessary variety in housing and the great range of production techniques needed to build it.[18]

In Britain it seems extraordinary that between a third and a half of the world's population still build their own homes, and that self-help accounts for 40 per cent of domestic building in Belgium, West Germany, Austria, Italy, France, Norway, Finland and Ireland. In Britain it is well under 10 per cent.[19] The difficulties people encounter when they set out to build for themselves are similar to those encountered by low-impact builders. This is due in part to the professionalization of knowledge that, as Ivan Illich argued, 'makes people dependent on having their knowledge produced for them' and leads to a paralysis of the moral and political imagination and, we have to say, of the *practical* imagination.[20] Creativity is supposed to be for the gifted few and the rest of us are compelled to live in environments constructed by them. Building upon this lie, says Simon Nicholson,

> the dominant cultural elite tell us that the planning, design and building of any part of the environment is so difficult and so special that only ... those with degrees and certificates in planning, engineering, architecture, art, education, behavioural psychology and so on – can properly solve environmental problems. The result is that the vast majority of people are not allowed (and worse – feel that they are incompetent) to experiment with the components of building.

The majority of the community has been deprived of a crucial part of their lives and lifestyle.[21]

The architect Christopher Day sought to enable communities to build for themselves through what he called consensus design. Day did not like the term 'empowerment', because he did not want the question of power to come into building at all. He did not think in terms of democracy because he did not believe in the right of the majority to impose its will on the minority. Nor did he believe in proceeding by debate because he felt people were not convinced by arguments. Instead, when given a settlement or a building he, with the group, looked at the place. Once the moods of a place are considered, he argued, concealed values started to emerge. From this emerges the spirit of a place. When consensus was reached on this he asked what the new development was to be about. From answers to this question emerged concrete practical details.[22]

Despite Day's objection I will continue to talk about empowerment, which calls for a revolution in the way we think about building houses. Day cites the example of the Lea View estate in Hackney where 90 per cent of the residents wanted to leave.

'Following intensive architect-resident collaboration, this socially and physically deprived community was turned into a place with positive community spirit. Vandalism, theft and muggings, formerly common, virtually disappeared; tenants' health improved, communal areas were looked after, and dignity and respect re-established. People now wanted to move on to the estate.' The identical estate next door, he notes, which was refurbished without tenant participation, reverted to a slum within six months.[23]

Alexander argues that building a house ought to be like having a child, and celebrated in the same kind of way. He calls for a more human operation in which the joy of building becomes paramount, in which the builders have a direct human relation to the work itself, to the houses, to the location of the houses, and to the people that the houses are for.[24] Improving design is not the issue. The alienated character of the buildings stems from the system of production, and it is this that needs changing.

From many points of view, therefore, the insight of the authors of Numbers, more than two millennia ago, needs to be central to the building of houses if those houses are to really meet human needs and doing this would be part and parcel of the social and political change that we also need if we are to survive.

The Priority of Beauty

Nicholas Wolterstorff remarks:

> The tragedy of modern urban life is not only that so many in our cities are oppressed and powerless, but also that so many have nothing surrounding them in which any human being could possibly take sensory delight. For this state of affairs we who are Christians are as guilty as any. We have adopted a pietistic-materialistic understanding of man, viewing human needs as the need for a saved soul plus the need for food, clothes and shelter. True shalom is vastly richer than that.[25]

That shalom includes 'something of the joy that rightfully belongs to human life, something of the satisfaction that aesthetically good housing would produce in those who dwell there'.[26] It is true that the aesthetic that derives from Scripture challenges most conventional aesthetics. God's glory is known in one in whom there is 'no form or majesty that we should look at him, nothing in his appearance that we should desire him' (Isa. 53.2). At the same time that glory is known, as I have already noted, in the radiant beauty of creation, which has from the earliest human origins called forth an answering human response. D. H. Lawrence was not entirely wrong when he said humans needed beauty more than they needed bread. Abbot Suger, the builder of Chartres; Aquinas, in his ruminations on the needs of the city (in *On Princely Government*); Abbot Alberti in his manifesto on architecture – all insisted that beauty was an essential aspect of the built environment springing from the 'claritas' or radiance that God is. But what does beauty mean in the houses that we build?

Christopher Day argues that it involves individuality and irregularity. Rows of rectangular buildings, he believes, oppress the freedom of the individual and, we can add, depress the spirit. In his own buildings he tries not to make one window the same as another:

> The vertebrae of the spine each carry a slightly different load and accept a slightly different movement. They are not identical. Each window likewise has an individual set of requirements to fulfil – unless we are just providing containers for people, albeit elaborate ones. It may be ridiculous to make every window different just for the sake of being different, but it is even more so to make every one the same just for the sake of being the same, or to shape them just to impose an elevational pattern.[27]

Day argues that the methods and materials of modern building militate against repose. 'In smooth plastered, gloss painted rooms you need a radio, hi-fi or television for company, to fill the empty space.'[28] Buildings can promote social and individual healing 'where the environment can offer interest, activity and intriguing ambiguity, timeless durability and a sense of roots (in place, past and future) in the wider natural world with its renewing rhythms, sociable places and relaxing atmospheres for the socially shy, and harmony, tranquillity and quiet soothing spaciousness'.[29] Much contemporary building is the equivalent of a diet of E numbers, which make people manic. He argues that we need a recovery of the sacred in the broadest sense, involving the ability of our senses to distinguish what is good for us and bad for us. Unless we are just providing containers for people, he remarks, we should have rooms that are congenial places for silence and meditation.

The recovery of the sacred involves the ability of our senses to tell us what is good or bad for us. Polyurethane-coated wood, for example, feels hard, smooth and cold and does not breathe. It looks like wood, but it is a lie and is bad food for the human spirit. 'If you want to bring children up to be honest it is not going to help if their environment is full of lies.'[30] At the same time, sick building syndrome is not just a matter of poor ventilation.[31] It has microbiological, chemical, thermal and electro biological dimensions. So, Day points out, formaldehyde is a highly reactive poison and carcinogen and is present in some varnishes, many glues, and includes products like chipboard, plywood and much furniture. Up to the middle of the twentieth century, he goes on, buildings were normally constructed of 30–40 per cent organic materials, and 60–70 per cent inorganic, including materials such as bricks, made from clay, and lime. Today many use 90–100 per cent artificial, synthetic materials. These may be easy to use but they can be harmful to health. According to Day, in our computerized world we are now exposed to electromagnetic radiation some 15,000 million times as strong as that which reaches us from the sun. Only recently, Day argues, has concern focused on the health consequences of upsetting the electrical, electrochemical and electromagnetic balances of the body. Short-term symptoms include headaches, weakness, disturbed sleep, nausea and loss of potency. More serious effects take years to show up. Various studies have suggested that up to 15 per cent of cancers in children and 90 per cent of infant deaths are related to electromagnetic fields. Buildings, Day states, should be seen as the third human skin (after the epidermis and clothing). The skin performs many functions: it breathes, absorbs, evaporates and regulates as well as enclosing and protecting. A building that, through its fabric, is in a constant state of moderated exchange between inside and outside feels – and is – a healthy place. It has a quality of life. A sealed-fabric building is full of dead air. Anybody who has lived in a vernacular house knows the difference between these and contemporary steel and concrete constructions, not to mention the cladding that sent Grenfell Tower up in flames. Health and beauty, it turns out, go together.

The Priority of Life

I have just mentioned the 'quality of life' in a building, and Day believes that the issue of life-full or life-less is at the heart of architecture.[32] John tells us that Jesus came that human beings should have 'life in all its fullness' (John 10.10), and in speaking of beautiful and healthy buildings I have already touched on that. But is there another sense in which buildings have life? I believe there is. Think of what happens when you go into a place and say, 'This is a lovely room', or when a house makes you feel more fully human, more at home in the world. Think of the contrast: rooms and houses that are oppressive, that you can't wait to get out of. What is going on here? Christopher Alexander's work over 40 years has tried to answer that question. He begins by trying to identify 'the quality without a name', a subtle kind of freedom from inner contradictions springing from an inner integrity. Something that has it is alive, has a self-maintaining fire; something that lacks it stifles life. For example, windows can bring to life or deaden. 'People are phototropic, tend towards the light, and, if you are in a room for any length of time you want to sit down. In that case well designed rooms have window seats or a place where you can draw up a chair. A room that has no window place, by contrast, in which the windows are just "holes", sets up an irresolvable inner conflict.'[33] The quality without a name is also free, not calculated or perfect but with a freedom that is generated from the forces of the material or the situation. It is eternal precisely in its ordinariness. In an insight close to Teresa of Avila or George Herbert he argues that 'the most mystical, most religious, most wonderful – these are not less ordinary than most things – they are more ordinary than most things. It is because they are so ordinary that they strike us to the core.'[34] This is illustrated by 'the simple rule that every room must have daylight on at least two sides (unless the room is less than eight feet deep)'. 'Rooms that follow this rule are pleasant to be in; rooms that do not follow it, with a few exceptions, are unpleasant to be in.'[35] Above all, the secret of the quality without a name is that it is egoless – a comment that resonates with much Christian reflection on sin and grace. Only this, he argues, allows a building to live. I have argued that there are analogies between the quality without a name and the idea of grace.[36] Forgetting Luke's stable and the homes that Jesus daily visited we tend to describe as 'gracious' or 'graceful' only the buildings of the extremely wealthy. Quite the opposite is true, as recognized in the dictum of the modernist architect Adolf Loos that the homes of peasants are formed by the hand of God.

Wrestling with these insights over 40 years – and building houses, including houses with (rather than for) the poor meanwhile – Alexander has been led to an extraordinary form of natural theology deriving from the built environment. Life, he argues, arises from a wholeness that lies under the surface of every place, at every time, in buildings, meadows, streets and so forth. To apprehend this wholeness we need to understand the theory of centres. A centre is 'a distinct set of points in space, which, because of its organization, because of its internal coherence, and because of its relation to context, exhibits centredness, forms a local zone of relative centredness with respect to the other parts of space'.[37] 'Life comes from the particular details of the ways the centres in the wholeness cohere to form a unity, the ways they interact, and interlock, and influence each other.'[38] That is the key to what is actually a metaphysical proposal: that life emerges through the inter-action of parts. It is a wholly relational view of reality. Centres are always made of other centres. A centre is not a point, not a perceived centre of gravity. 'It is rather a field of organized force in an object or part of an object that makes that object or part exhibit centrality. This field like centrality is fundamental to the idea of wholeness.'[39] Alexander argues that what we call material reality is alive because of its structure, and because of its geometry. 'What is alive, is the earth, and rock, and space itself. The life includes the air, again inorganic. It is not life in space, not an inorganic mechanical substrate, filled with a few living organisms. It is one living thing, the space has come to life, it is nonsense to separate the two.'[40] Life is something that exists in every event and building, even in everyday functional life as a consequence of the structure of space. The actual substance out of which the environment is made consists of relations, or patterns, not things; and it is actually generated by the implicit, language-like system of rules that determines the structure.[41]

Reality, then – or 'nature' – is a living structure but life depends on the relation of centres. This is not an automatic thing for order is distinct from beauty:

> Many of the ugliest patterns and most joyless buildings – buildings from which no being can ever have derived delight – possess order in a high degree. Instances of this among the hideous flats, warehouses and other commercial buildings of our streets require no citation. Here is Order and no beauty, but, on the contrary, ugliness.[42]

There are living and dead places and the artist and the archi-tect are charged with helping structures come to life. 'The nature of space matter, being soul like, is such that the more whole it becomes ... the more it realizes itself, releases its own inner reality.' Because this is the case, and because art is about building and shaping, 'it has an importance that goes to the very core of cosmology'. 'The task of building things and shaping things is fundamental to the spiritual condition of the world and to our own spiritual development. It is our closest approach, almost God like, to creating life, and to seeing and reaching the essential core of things.'[43]

This takes Alexander on to theological reflection:

> To make living structure – really to make living structure – it seems almost as though somehow, we are charged, for our time, with finding a new form of god, a new way of understanding the deepest origins of our experience, of the matter in the universe so that we, too, when lucky, with devotion, might find it possible to reveal this 'something' and its blinding light.[44]

In his view – and I think there is an analogy with the gothic builders here – when we encounter harmony in things or people 'then spirit is made real'. The underlying spirit of the world becomes visible. 'We are then face to face with God. This quality, when it appears in things, people, in a moment, in an event, is God. It is not an indication of God living behind all things, but it actually is God itself. That is spirit made manifest.'[45] There is an analogy here to the claim that God can be known in the experience of grace, whether in the Eucharist, in a relationship, or in a place. *Ubi gratia ibi Deus est.*

This is, of course, a natural theology, and as a Barthian of the most unreconstructed kind I cannot simply embrace it, but I do think that Alexander is calling Christians to take up aspects of their tradition to which they have allowed themselves to become blind. The NAME creates all things except those that are evil, loves all things except those that are evil, is present to all things, whether evil or not. The house, the place where human beings dwell, is called to respond to grace and to reflect it. When it does that, it is alive and fosters fullness of life. When we turn away from grace, let ego take over, we produce life-denying places, places unworthy for human beings to dwell.

Once More: Agenda 21

As a species we now top 8 billion, and will probably exceed UN expectations by 2100. All these billions need places to live that will not destroy the planet, and that will preserve the fertile soil that feeds us. It should be clear that this goal cannot be met by handing building over to the volume builders. All the Lord's people must be prophets; all, like the population of Nehemiah's Jerusalem, must play their part; all must learn to live in a low-impact way, for the sake of others and for the sake of the future. And all, in response to God's gracious, ecstatic and beautiful self-gift, must seek to form places of the soul, places of beauty and life. That was what the Deuteronomists wanted in their command to 'seek life' (Deut. 30.19).

Notes

1 Gorringe, T. J. (2004), *A Theology of the Built Environment*, Cambridge: Cambridge University Press, p. 1.

2 Rodger, A. (1996), 'Sustainable Development, Energy Policy Issues and Greenhouse', in Samuels, R. and Prasad, D., *Global Warming and the Built Environment*, London: Spon, p. 96.

3 Smith, M., Whiteleg, J. and Williams, N. (1998), *Greening the Built Environment*, London: Earthscan, p. 6.

4 Smith, Whiteleg and Williams, *Greening*, p. 42.

5 Haughton, G. and Hunter, C. (1994), *Sustainable Cities*, London: Regional Studies Association, p. 14.

6 Fairlie, S. (1996), *Low Impact Development*, Charlbury: Jon Carpenter, p. 51.

7 Fairlie, *Low*, p. 60.

8 Ruskin, J. (1989), *The Seven Lamps of Architecture*, New York: Dover (orig. 1880), p. 171.

9 McCamant, K. and Durrett, C. (1994), *Cohousing: A Contemporary Approach to Housing Ourselves*, Berkeley, CA: TenSpeed Press, p. 145.

10 Ward, C. (1985), *When We Build Again*, London: Pluto, p. 83.

11 Wates, N. and Knevitt, C. (1987), *Community Architecture*, Harmondsworth: Penguin, p. 122.

12 Wates and Knevitt, *Community*, p. 155.

13 I have tried to explore this in relation to the global emergency

in *The World Made Otherwise: Sustaining Humanity in a Threatened World* (2018), Eugene, OR: Cascade Books.

14 Alexander, C. (1979), *The Timeless Way of Building*, New York: Oxford University Press, p. 164.

15 Alexander, *Timeless*, p. 236.

16 Turner, J. F. C. (1976), *Housing by People: Towards Autonomy in Building Environments*, London: Marion Boyars, p. 62.

17 Turner, J. F. C. and Fichter, R., eds (1972), *Freedom to Build: Dweller Control of the Housing Process*, London: Macmillan, p. 241.

18 Turner and Fichter, *Freedom*, p. 83.

19 It is still, however, 12,000 homes a year (Fairlie, *Low*, p. 94).

20 Cited in Ward, C. (1996), *Talking to Architects*, London: Freedom, p. 20.

21 Cited in Ward, *Talking*, p. 23.

22 Day, C. (2003), *Consensus Design: Socially Inclusive Process*, Oxford: Architectural Press, ch 7.

23 Day, *Consensus*, pp. 12, 14.

24 Alexander, C., with H. Davis, J. Martinez and D. Corner (1985), *The Production of Houses*, New York: Open University Press, p. 298.

25 Wolterstorff, N. (1997), *Art in Action*, Carlisle: Solway, p. 82.

26 Wolterstorff, *Art*, p. 170.

27 Day, C. (1999), *Places of the Soul*, London: Thorsons, p. 90.

28 Day, *Places*, p. 142.

29 Day, *Places*, p. 26.

30 Day, *Places*, p. 51.

31 For what follows, see Day, *Places*, ch. 4.

32 Day, *Places*, p. 43.

33 Alexander, *Timeless*, p. 111.

34 Alexander, *Timeless*, p. 219.

35 Alexander, *Timeless*, p. 220.

36 Gorringe, T. J. (2011), *The Common Good and the Global Emergency*, Cambridge: Cambridge University Press, ch. 3.

37 Alexander, C. (2002), *The Phenomenon of Order*, Berkeley, CA: Center for Environmental Structure, p. 84.

38 Alexander, *Phenomenon*, p. 106.

39 Alexander, *Phenomenon*, p. 118.

40 Alexander, *Phenomenon*, p. 430.

41 Grabow, S. (1983), *Christopher Alexander: The Search for a New Paradigm in Architecture*, Stocksfield: Oriel, p. 45.

42 Scott, G. (1956), *The Architecture of Humanism: A Study in the History of Taste*, 2nd edn, New York: Doubleday (orig. 1924) p. 155.

43 Alexander, C. (2002), *The Luminous Ground*, Berkeley, CA: Center for Environmental Structure, p. 331.

44 Alexander, *Luminous Ground*, p. 42.

45 Alexander, *Luminous Ground*, p. 302.

3

Space and Neighbours

STEPHEN BACKHOUSE

This book aims to shine a light on some of the deep Christian theology at work in the world of housing, resource management and community development.

When the Church offers its opinion on housing practice and policy it is not meddling in affairs peripheral to Christian life and thought. It is drawing from wells that nourished the earliest followers of Christ, and which fed the political imagination of people who saw themselves as citizens of the kingdom formed around Jesus. Concern for the right ordering of human life that leads to human flourishing is not an optional extra on the edges of the gospel. It forms the beating heart at its centre.

We want to provide language for concepts and activities that *anyone* involved in tackling the housing crisis will encounter. To be concerned with housing is to deal with *land and space* management and the creation and maintenance of *neighbourhoods*.

Fortunately, Christians do not have to invent new terms for these concepts and activities. How Christians negotiate the spheres of *space* and *neighbours* are some of the oldest Christian ideas in existence.

By 'neighbours' we mean specifically the people living near and next to us. Here we need to account for what constitutes a neighbourhood, and how this can be differentiated from other forms of human grouping. When we look at our neighbours we are looking at issues of identity, belonging, responsibility, peace and conflict. The preferential emphasis that Christians place on neighbourhoods over and against nationhoods is discussed in the section 'Neighbourhood not Nationhood' on page 45. First, though, we will turn our attention to the Christian business of managing space.

'Gentle Space Making'

'Space' here refers to the patches of land on which any house is built, and also to the spheres in which habitants must live and move. The word as used here means land and land management, and also internal architecture, planning and habitation. When we talk about the building of houses we talk about 'land grabs', 'making space', 'opening up space', 'preserving space'. When we describe the business of living in houses we talk about 'room to breathe' or 'swing a cat', 'space to move', 'a room of one's own', 'being crowded out', and so on.

The management of space is thus a private matter, a social affair and a political problem. What is often overlooked, however, even by Christians, is that there is a deep *theology* around the business of managing space. The aim of this section is to describe one of the key ideas at the heart of the Christian imagination. *Kenosis* is the Greek word used to describe the 'self-emptying' of Jesus Christ. *Kenosis* is not fundamentally a spiritual or religious word, though, but rather a practical, moral and political one. As will be discussed below, this concept gives Christians a vocabulary for the practice of 'gentle space making' and provides a helpful tool in the business of recognizing and enabling personal flourishing in the spaces for which they bear some responsibility. Such a practice is not new to the Church. Indeed, an attitude of 'gentle space making' is about as anciently Christian as it is possible to get, pre-dating even the Gospels.[1]

The four Gospels are not the first words anyone wrote about Jesus. Mark, Matthew, Luke and John are accounts written down and stitched together a generation or two after the events they are describing. The people who knew Jesus were dying, so the people who knew the people who knew Jesus preserved their stories. The Church was already in existence for a generation or more before it had four biographical accounts of the words and life of its founder. For the best indication of what it felt like to be around Jesus we have to turn to earlier sources. Here we find the epistles and letters that make up the bulk of the New Testament, most of which are ascribed to the Apostle Paul. Paul's letters, it is worth reminding ourselves, were written for and about people who had living memory of Jesus. And Paul, it is also worth noting, was not always writing new material. He often quotes sayings of Jesus or teachings of the first disciples that were well known to his contemporaries. And, in one notable passage in his epistle to the congregation in the city of Philippi, Paul incorporates a poem into his text that he probably did not originally pen.

A political song

This 'hymn', found in Philippians 2, thus has a credible claim to being one of the earliest things ever written about Jesus, by people within living memory of what it felt like to be around him. It is worth quoting in full:

> Let each of you look not only to his own interests, but also to the interests of others. Have this mind among yourselves, which is yours in Christ Jesus, who, though he was in the form of God, did not count equality with God a thing to be grasped, but emptied himself, by taking the form of a servant, being born in the likeness of men. And being found in human form, he humbled himself by becoming obedient to the point of death, even death on a cross. Therefore God has highly exalted him and bestowed on him the name that is above every name, so that at the name of Jesus every knee should bow, in heaven and on earth and under the earth, and every tongue confess that Jesus Christ is Lord, to the glory of God the Father. (Phil. 2.4–11)

The history of interpretation of this passage is dominated by pundits speculating about its contribution to Trinitarian doctrine, as if it was primarily a philosophical exploration of how the divine could become human. But Philippians is not trying to describe the unique theological relationship of the Godhead. This makes nonsense of Paul's assumption that the hymn contains something that his readers can emulate ('have this mind among yourselves'). Instead, this passage initially describes how Jesus as a powerful human lived and how he used his power. And, as we shall see, it suggests how people, emulating the divine Jesus, can posture themselves individually and communally in such a way as to allow room for others to grow, rather than wither on the vine.

Two thousand years of tin ears has led us to overlook how overtly *socio-political* this hymn is.[2] The passage is directly applicable to the everyday world of human organization of power and its distribution, as its original readers would have known full well. Not for nothing is the hymn inserted into a letter to a Church primarily riven apart by faulty approaches to authority and conflict resolution.

The first clue that we are in the realm of socio-politics is the Greek phrase *isa theo* ('equality with God'). *Isa theo* is not a 'religious' statement, if, by that, you think that the religious and the political can be easily separated. In the Greco-Roman imagination, the more powerful a person was, the more of a little god they were. It is the phrase Augustus used when he threw his hat into the ring to become Caesar. It is the phrase used of people gunning for the top job of 'king of the world'. And it is the phrase that the earliest Christians thought was most appropriate for describing what it felt like to be around Jesus as he pronounced the coming of a new kingdom and formed a new movement of followers around him. Significantly, in this hymn, people being 'equal to God' is not the problem. It is *how* they go about achieving this power that is being subverted.

Jesus was equal to God, but he did not consider being equal to God a matter of 'grasping' or 'exploiting for his own advantage'. The Greek word in view here is another technical political term: *harpagmon*. This is the garnering of political resources and directing them towards getting what you want. If you have ever been asked to sign a petition or join a protest rally, you have been on the pointy end of *harpagmon*. When politicians gather together their 'base' or canvas support they are hoovering power in order to use it to their own advantage when the crunch time comes. This is the way politics works. You grasp at what power you can find in order to shape the world according to your vision and the vision of those who have pledged their support. *Harpagmon* is a matter of grasping and focusing in order to dominate your 'will'.

Yet Jesus, who is *isa theo*, does not consider *isa theo* a matter of *harpagmon*. Instead, insist the people who knew him, he 'emptied himself'. *Kenosis*. And with this, we come to *space*.

Following priest and theologian Sarah Coakley, to practise *kenosis* is to practise 'gentle space making'. To 'empty oneself' is not to become a doormat or a cringing worm. Imagine a bathtub with water pouring out of the taps. We all know that water flows to fill the space. Now imagine if the running water could willingly put a limit on its movement. What if it stopped halfway through? We would observe that rather than self-filling, it is self-emptying. In human terms, to be a kenotic person is to practise self-control of your will. Tyrants and bullies (and, let's be honest, many celebrities, businesspeople and politicians) fill the space with their egos. As the powerful person enters the room all eyes turn, all conversations cease, and all ideas are bent to that person. Whether intentional or not, *harpagmon* kicks in as the dominant person gathers and subsumes other wills in the service of their own will. Practitioners of *harpagmon* close down dissent, conversation and divergence.

By contrast, imagine a powerful person entering a room, but instead of flowing to fill the space they stand quietly to the side, listening to the different conversations around them. That person then approaches one individual and, noticing a connection they have with another, brings the two strangers into conversation and friendship. Would anyone think such a person was a cringing worm? Of course not. But by managing their ego and taking responsibility to cultivate the space they find themselves in, our powerful person has demonstrated *kenosis*. The *kenotic* person practises 'gentle space making' by limiting their self to make room for other selves. To be like a servant is not to be servile. A prime mark of a servant is that they exist to enable other people. The *kenotic* person enacts 'emptiness' in so far as they take responsibility for their power and do not let it dominate the space. They serve other 'wills', and by so doing allow other people to flourish.

It is this quality that the earliest Christians identified with their powerful leader, Jesus the Christ, and it was this quality that they themselves sought to emulate as they managed and organized the spaces they found themselves in. Crucial Christian practices such as servant leadership, forgiveness, mutual submission, laying down your life for your friends and treating others better than yourselves cannot be understood apart from *kenosis*.

Kenosis is about conflict resolution, political postures and managing social spaces. For this reason a further implication of *kenosis* is that it leads to a proliferation of 'persons'. When one makes gentle space by withdrawing their will, the immediate effect is that other wills are allowed to bloom. *Kenotic* spaces are spaces where people are not thwarted but thrive.

Philippians is not the only place we find Jesus practising gentle space making that leads to the flourishing of other people. Every time he engages foreigners or women (or, in the case of the Samaritan at the well, both at the same time!) he is making space for other opinions and voices that were not normally allowed to be heard. These are not simply theoretical spaces: they are physical and geographical too. Samaritans lived in villages that a Jewish Rabbi was not supposed to set foot in. An interesting example of *kenosis* in action is the famous story in Mark 5 of the woman with menstrual bleeding who touches Jesus' cloak in order to be healed. We are told that the crowd is pressing around, but at the moment of her action, Jesus stops the throng and demands to know who touched him. By this stage in the Gospel we are well acquainted with a man who knows men's minds and hearts. Jesus is not presented as someone who needs to ask questions to know information about others. So why now? The answer lies in seeing his question as not for his benefit, but hers. The immediate effect of his stopping the crowd and asking his pointed question is that the woman had to step forward. Here is a woman with no one to speak for her, trapped in a crushing cycle of loneliness, illness and poverty. According to the common sense of her culture, she was the lowest of the low – more unclean on the purity scale than a dead animal. She was, for all intents and purposes, less than human. Jesus could have identified her himself with a word and gesture of authority, demonstrating yet again his overriding power in the sphere. And yet, by creating the time and the space for her to come out and speak, Jesus created the conditions to make visible who was unseen, to make heard who had no voice. And to the woman who had no family and no champion he gives an identity: 'Daughter your faith has healed you' (Mark 5.34). In short, much like God who practises *kenosis* in Genesis 1, by creating space for other wills to exist from nothing, Jesus self-limits and, by so doing, creates a 'person' where before there was none.

In terms of business and the politics of housing, *kenosis* is a supremely useful concept for Christians: both in their ability to observe and describe situations around them, and also as a guide to action when followers of Christ find themselves in positions of power and responsibility. Self-control, kindness and hospitality are all fruits of the Spirit, and all are underwritten by *kenosis*. Likewise, any political act or social space we encounter that creates the conditions for human flourishing is a *kenotic* space. A lively sense of 'gentle space making' also provides us with the ability to recognize and diagnose its opposite: *harpagmon*. Exploitation and hoarding that leads to domination and thwarting of others' wills is as easy to find in social spaces as it is in the human heart. Talk of hoarding power or giving it away, of crowded or open environments, and their relation to human freedom and flourishing, are all concepts crucial to the housing crisis. And they are all found in the New Testament. Managing space well is as deeply Christian as it is possible to get.

Having 'gentle space making' in mind provides Christian planning officers and policy makers a much needed moral compass in a notoriously complex and ideologically confused field where individual lives are often overlooked at the expense of massive budgets and partisan loyalty. At the wider policy level, a lively sense of their mission as 'gentle space makers' provides Christians with a language for diagnosing malign forms of public policy that thwart living space, hoard resources, or bull-doze over the wills of the many in favour of the wills of the few. Living conditions that do not enable their inhabitants to thrive, communities that are squeezed for space, neighbourhoods threatened by commercial concerns, or local housing groups seeking to have their voice heard in the midst of powerful indus-trial or political systems, are all commonplace occurrences in the world of housing policy. And all can be described with reference to *kenosis* and its opposite, *harpagmon*.

The second key overlap between housing and Christian the-ology is that both are intimately concerned with the creation and maintenance of neighbourhoods.

Neighbourhood Not Nationhood

The Church of England, for understandable reasons, feels it has a stake in the ongoing conversation of what it means to be 'English'. Likewise, any exploration of 'the housing crisis' in the UK will invariably need to address the variations of the matter across Wales, Scotland, Northern Ireland and England.

But there is a trap here, glittering and shiny, which – if we are not careful – will capture our imaginations and usurp the conversation. For the housing crisis is not going to be solved by focusing on 'the nation'. It is only going to make sense if we understand it as affecting 'the neighbour'. Christian theology has a gift to bring to the table, and that is the understanding that the neighbour is a more important category than the national.

Neighbourhoods are not simply nationhoods writ large. Neighbourhoods are particular, while nations are abstract. When it comes to defining the identity of the real persons around which we have to live and work, national identity is imprecise, prone to sentimental love or hate, ever changing, endlessly definable. If we see everyone as – fundamentally – a neighbour, however, we have access to a category that does not first force us to establish their authentic bona fides before we can determine our attitude towards them. It is not for nothing that Jesus counselled his people to love their neighbours, a category of identity that he explicitly defined over and against the category of the nation.

A *tale of two groups*

There are two main ways to imagine our relationships to other people and groups. Let us call one 'the herd' and the other 'the neighbourhood'. Both have their good points and their uses. Both are human and natural. They can look very similar to the untrained eye. But they are not equal, for they are based on fundamentally different starting points. [3]

'Herds' are arranged on a *like for like* principle. Here, individuals group with other people who are as much like them as possible. Sports fans, hobby groups, political parties, tribes and nations are all 'herds' in so much as they are formed by people who share passions or characteristics in common with one another. The healthiness of the herd is based on each individual cultivating and protecting this 'alikeness'. The guiding attitude of the herd is that relationship is based on everyone being as much like everyone else as possible. Individuals who stop supporting the local team, fall out of love with a hobby, marry a foreigner, vote for the other side, or love another country (or none) will naturally test the limits of the herd and their membership will rightly be called into question. Individuals with a herd mentality say to themselves, 'I need to relate to people who look like me, think like me, or act like me as much as possible.' This is a deeply human, historical and natural impulse. It is the way most human organizations at any level are formed.

'Neighbourhood' relationships are also natural and human, but they are arranged on the *unlike for unlike* principle. Here, the relationship is not in its essence based on shared interests, skin colour, accent, religion and politics, etc., but by geography and mutual awareness. A neighbourhood is a looser collection of individuals who are not congregating around what ideological or physical features they have in common, but by the fact that they share the same space, and are alert to one another's presence. Neighbourhoods are not as strongly bound together as tribes or factions, but they cover more ground. Your neighbour is not defined by any passion that they share in common with you. They are identified because they are next to you, when they impinge on your consciousness, or lay claim to your responsibility.

The network of neighbourhood relationships is bigger than that of herd relationships. In other words, if I become aware of my responsibility towards a person who hates my hobbies, is opposed to my politics, disbelieves my religion, is not of my tribe and does not speak my language, they may not be in my herd, but they are still my neighbour.

Neighbourhood relations are not as exciting, passionate, sentimental or compelling as herd relations. In a contest of what pulls on the heartstrings, history suggests the herd wins every time.

Yet it is the neighbour – and not the herd – who Jesus commands his followers to love. Indeed, the parable of the Good Samaritan in Luke 10 is founded precisely on contrasting 'herd' with 'neighbour'. The outsider helping a hated foreigner lying in the ditch is the model of authentic love. For all that the priest and Levite shared the victim's religion, nationality, language and politics, they ultimately prove themselves as individuals unable to demonstrate love. Note that it is not being a Levite or a Jewish priest that is so bad (or indeed that being a Samaritan is so good), it is that the herd mentality is incapable of producing the kind of person who can love others the way God desires us to love.

Authentic identity, authentic love

Authentic identity is essential for human flourishing. You cannot grow into the person you are meant to be if you are rooted in the wrong soil. Identity that is not rooted in God *cannot* be authentic because it is not rooted in the One in whom we live and move and have our being (Acts 17.28). Christianly we say that if self-identity is founded on anything other than God, then it is a form of idolatry. This very much includes attempts to form a sense of authentic self-hood based on self-love and self-affirmation that is generated from within. As a Christian I recognize that my authentic individual identity comes from Another, and not from me. A sense of self that is based on one's *own self* being the highest authority is monstrous.

There is a tendency towards selfishness inherent in 'herd love'. We have said that herds are based on the 'like for like' principle. Here, likeminded people need to remain likeminded if they are to remain in relationship with one another. The love that is shared in these groups can be passionate, strong, brave and true, but it is also always partial and provisional. Herd love puts limits on who counts as 'in' and who is 'out' because it needs to. The more one can be seen to share the characteristics or instincts of the others, the more real the love is. We do not expect sports fans to love *all* teams equally, or patriots to love *all* countries equally. That would undermine the very point of the love being expressed. We love particular groups with particular characteristics *because* of those particular characteristics. To be clear: not all the love generated by herds is wrong and not all herds are bad. It is simply to say that herds are very good at producing individuals who are very good at herd love. But the one thing that they cannot do is produce humans who are very good at 'neighbour love'.

This is where the tendency to 'selfishness' comes in. If my mantra as an individual is 'I need to relate to people who look like me, think like me, or act like me as much as possible', then the ultimate horizon of such a movement is . . . *me*. When my love is based on how much others are like me, *I* become the judge, jury and executioner of who is worthy of my love and

48

who is allowed to lay claim to my affections. The problem with herd love is that despite its appearance of being about other people, in fact it is ultimately and literally 'self-centred'. People group into herds because of how much the herd reflects their characteristics back to them. When I am in a herd I find it easy to exclude others, or push them away from relationship, because it is easy to identify when another individual does not share my features, values or passions. Not only is self-centredness like this an unhealthy basis for love for other people, it is also a bad foundation for self-identity because it is based on an idol. This is the opposite trajectory demanded by the love that Jesus talks about, and on which the earliest local expressions of the Church were founded.

Thus, when it comes to analysing human issues on a national scale, we only do ourselves a disservice when we assume that the 'national' strand is the most important aspect of human identity and coordinate our outlook accordingly by reducing what is most important about a person to one – and only one – group that they might belong to. Rather than operating in the abstract, Christians would do well to engage with people as they really are. This includes the ever-changing complexity of what it means to be a human being. Fortunately, Christians have a word for describing a person in such a way that their individuality is preserved in all its elements without reducing their identity to any one element and without reference to any groups they might belong to. And that word is 'neighbour'.

Love thy neighbour

If the Christian duty is to love, then there must be a target of that love, and a better or worse way of identifying that target (as the young lawyer who asked Jesus 'who is my neighbour?' in Luke 10 knew full well). There is a tension underlying the duty to love, and that is the determination of who or what constitutes the focus of our responsibility: is it those who share the same formational culture, the formational culture itself, or a 'person' whose definition transcends these socialized models?

If a person must be properly socialized in order to be considered a 'person', then in effect only those who share one's socio-political context are 'persons' when it comes to identifying the targets of ethical duty. But if there is something above and beyond shared preferences that make a person a person, then that has implications for who and how we should love.

A common fear is that to move away from focus on the nation is to move away from concrete reality and towards a vague sentiment that is utopian, unworkable and, ultimately, inhuman. But in fact the opposite is true. Neighbour love is better than nation love precisely *because* it is realistic, creaturely and local. Problems with basing practical ethical action on national identity arise not because it is focused on the stuff of this life, but because it excludes so many people, withdrawing into tighter and tighter circles of sameness, and thus abstraction away from reality.

Neighbour love has a further advantage over herd or nation love in that the identification of the subject to be loved is infinitely simpler. Herd love (as with all national/patriotic affections) needs to draw up endless distinctions and exclusions, in order to attain the purest expression of its passion. For example, libraries, academic conferences and journal articles devote much time and space to the subject of defining national identity and patriotic allegiance. There is no similar space devoted to 'neighbour'. This is because that person's identity is not in question. Kierkegaard remarks that when one is searching for one's neighbour, all one needs to do is open the door and go out. 'The very first person you meet is the neighbour, whom you *shall* love . . . There is not a single person in the whole world who is as surely and as easily recognized as the neighbour.'[4]

Kierkegaard's 'neighbour' is a cipher for other individuals: the 'I' whose existence can be affirmed without reference to oneself and without making an appeal to the slippery notion of the nation. I want to highlight here how it is that the neighbour is an alternative Christian category that undermines the confidence normally placed in the commonsensical category of the 'compatriot'. As a way of describing the recipient or target of our love, the neighbour competes with – and subverts – the compatriot. 'Neighbours' are real and concrete in a way that a person identified primarily along 'national' lines can never be.

This is not to say that 'neighbours' rescind their respective national identities, only that the total of their identity as persons is not summed up by their national story. Or, to put it another way, in the real societies in which we live, the individuals around us may or may not be our compatriots, but they will always be our neighbours. The Christian does not have an ethical duty only towards people whose national narratives dovetail with their own – the duty is to love the neighbour simply *because* they are the neighbour.[5]

Arguably, only that which looks outward, and engages with other persons regardless of their similarity to us, can properly be deemed *love*. A social life based on infatuation for the group is far less useful to members of that society than one based on practical regard for others. True sociality cannot be based on affection for the nation, trumped up and maintained by self-serving fictions. It must be directed instead at the existing subject in the here and now.

In sum, what Christians bring to any national conversation about neighbours is the realization that, when it comes to loving others as they truly are, neighbourhoods are bigger, more real, and a more important category to Jesus than nationhoods will ever be. In terms of the business and policy of housing, the Christian concept of the importance of 'neighbours' should obviously underwrite their commitment to the construction of neighbourhoods. Much like the language of 'gentle space making', a high value for the neighbour will aid the Christian in positively identifying when a collection of people is a mere group of houses and when they are in neighbourly relations with one another. On the critical side, the realization that 'the neighbour' is a more important category than 'the nation' will provide Christians with the theological ammunition needed to resist populist turns towards nationalism which increasingly dominate the conversation when it comes to who is and who isn't a legitimate person in our society. Christians need to resist grounding their housing policy on appeals to 'Englishness' or sentimental patriotism. Nationalism is a tawdry substitute for real love of real persons. As Kierkegaard says: 'Love for neighbour does not want to be sung about – it wants to be accomplished.'[6]

Notes

1 The literature on *kenosis* and Philippians 2 is voluminous. For the political background to the *kenotic* hymn, see especially the chapter by E. M. Heen, in Horsely, R., ed. (2004), *Paul and the Roman Imperial Order*, London: Trinity Press International.

2 The phrase is Sarah Coakley's. See her chapter 'Kenosis and Subversion', in Coakley, S. (2006), *Powers and Submissions: Spirituality, Philosophy and Gender*, Oxford: Blackwell Publishing.

3 Much of the following observations on love, individuals and groups are indebted to the Danish philosopher and theologian Søren Kierkegaard (1813–55). He claimed his aim was 'to reintroduce Christianity into Christendom' in his book *Works of Love* (2009, London: Harper-Collins), which is an extended reflection on Jesus' commands to love God and love neighbour.

4 Kierkegaard, *Works*, pp. 51–2.

5 Kierkegaard, *Works*, p. 55. Following the parable of the Good Samaritan the neighbour is not the one who shares the same cultural markers as the one in need. It is the foreigner who is aware of the need and does something about it.

6 Kierkegaard, *Works*, p. 46.

4

Housing, Church, Community – and Christian Theology

MALCOLM BROWN

Theology and Housing

Houses have to be built somewhere – and so they must stand in relation to their wider surroundings and context. But while there is a significant theological literature about the spiritual significance of 'place', and even more on the nature of good communities, cities and so on, there is surprisingly little on housing itself. Yet a house is, so to speak, the vehicle through which people become located within specific places and communities. A house is the material frame within which that proto-community, the family, forms, is nurtured and grows. Houses create spaces for privacy, sleep, hospitality and security – all essential aspects of a balanced life. And the relationship of houses to other houses creates a framework for neighbourliness that can help balance the inherent tension in humanity's need to assert both the individual and the community as fundamental facets of our existence. The moral philosopher Alasdair MacIntyre uses the shorthand 'dependent, rational animals' to signify the human condition – and the way we construct and inhabit houses can serve to facilitate – or to frustrate – our dependency on others, our animal need for company, solitude and sustenance, and our God-given ability to think, to plan and to theorize about how we live and then to put those thoughts into practice.[1]

Architecture matters. Some great houses seem designed to

project worldly power, wealth and control over those who surround them. Some stress individualism and privacy to the extent that they seem to deny any mutuality between their occupants and others. Some make so little provision for privacy that people feel as if they live under permanent threat from unknown others. The way houses are built speaks volumes about our collective care and sympathy (or lack of those virtues) for the global environment. The way they are situated in relation to one another is deeply expressive of what we believe about the ways people should relate to one another. Identical houses built in rows offer a different account of what is important about a community compared to, say, clusters of more individual houses arranged in squares or around court-yards.[2] The semiotics of high-rise housing has generated a considerable literature of its own. So there is plenty of theo-logical raw material for addressing questions about housing.

Housing and Home in Scripture

If we take 'housing' to mean something more permanent than a tent or temporary shelter, Scripture is ambiguous about per-manent settlement. Consequent upon the Fall, Adam and Eve are banished from the Garden where their material needs were effortlessly provided and have to fend for themselves. In the deepest sense, they have lost their home and the security of their whole habitation is brought into jeopardy. Throughout Scripture, the true home of humanity is understood to be in unity with God, and the characteristics of a home – some of which are made real by being incorporated in a physical dwell-ing place – are to be found in the peace, but most of all in the relationships, that being in God's presence implies. 'Our hearts are restless until they find their rest in You' (Augustine). The curse invoked upon Adam is that he will be a rootless person, deprived of that fundamental relationship with his maker – 'you will be a fugitive and a wanderer on the earth' (Gen. 4.12). To be homeless, in this profound sense, is intrinsic to human-ity's fallen condition. The subsequent history of humanity's relationship to God, in the Old and the New Testaments, is about the continuing tension between our fallenness and the constant activity of God to draw us back to himself – to re-establish the human home in a renewed at-one-ment. Given the centrality of this tension between rootedness and rootless-ness, it is not surprising that the Bible should, on the face of it, have little to say about houses but much to say about the contrasts between nomadic and settled lives. This reveals the risk that too much investment in permanence might detract from an awareness of God's continuing saving activity and the necessity of being alert to the call to uproot and respond to intimations of God's love.

Paradigmatic, in the Old Testament, is the story of Abraham, setting off from Ur of the Chaldeans in search of a promised land (Gen. 12.1). Tracing the lineage of the whole people of Israel back to Abraham immediately makes disturbance from settled routines central to identity under God. The beginnings of redemption from the Fall occur when Abraham follows the call to take up God's promise of a land in which the people can settle again. Not a return to Eden itself, but the beginnings of a covenantal relationship with God that marks some restoration of the Fall's estrangement. For a nomadic people, housing is, of necessity, temporary – something one can carry around on a journey and that is essentially context-free, and as much a 'house' in one location as another.

But, over time, the nomadic imperative will be succeeded by arrival in the promised land and the close identification of a particular people with a particular place. This is a culmin-ation of the insight that God is an imminent God, active in shaping the world and human affairs, and revealed not just in a general presence but in a specific identification with specific places and times. It is not that God is any more present in one place than another, but that human awareness of that presence is associated with moments and places that take on an intense theological significance. Throughout the Old Testament, places are named to commemorate moments when the presence of God has been felt especially intensely or dramatically. Once place takes on a divine significance, human habitation linked to significant places becomes more permanent – or, more to the point, people's sense that their identity under God is formed by place leads to a more lasting sense of belonging to places. Yet movement and relocation are always lurking possibilities in the lives of the faithful and God's encounters with his people often take place at moments of dislocation. Jacob's dream takes place while he is travelling and far from home (Gen. 28.10–15). Impermanence is never far away in the scriptural narratives, and this is true for the more settled communities as well as for the years of wandering.

The Ark of the Covenant, which had accompanied the people through their wanderings, comes to rest in Jerusalem as the focal point and raison d'etre of the temple. This semi-permanence is not without controversy (2 Sam. 7). But it marks the early consciousness that not only the promised land itself, but even more the great city of Jerusalem, are particular focal points for God's presence in the world. The human city becomes imbued with some of the characteristics of heaven itself – God's particular, but not unique, dwelling place. The human city becomes, at some level, a theological construction and the way people (and peoples) build cities, including houses and public spaces, moves beyond questions of utility and survival to carry symbolic and theological meanings constructed in stone, wood and earth.

The focus on Jerusalem, of course, adds a deep poignancy to the later exile of the people in Babylon. And here we pick up one of the rare moments in Scripture where the building of houses is shown to be part of God's plan. The prophet Jeremiah's letter to the exiles states explicitly:

Build houses and live in them; plant gardens and eat what they produce. Take wives and have sons and daughters . . . seek the welfare of the city where I have sent you into exile, and pray to the LORD on its behalf, for in its welfare you will find your welfare. (Jer. 29.5–8)

The theme of exile – of being separated from our true home in God – recurs throughout the Gospels and the rest of the New

Testament (this theme needs fleshing out . . .). But so does the prophetic image of seeking the welfare of the city in which one is exiled. To cut a long story very short (!), herein lies a fundamental tension at the heart of Christian ethics – the fact that we are called to live as if Christ is returning tomorrow while nonetheless investing strongly in the future of the world in which we find ourselves 'resident aliens' (1 Pet. 1.6).[3] This is part of our mandate to work with the compromises and contingencies of the world in order to advance a kingdom that we know will not be completed until Christ returns.

The exile theme, in Old and New Testaments, has important implications for the ways we conceive and construct human community – and for the contribution the built environment makes to that vocation. As resident aliens, bidden to seek the welfare of the city around us, our human communities are simultaneously crucial and contingent. It is vital to have a place to belong – but to know that it is not our ultimate place of belonging. Might we extend that insight to housing questions by suggesting that houses need to be well built and well located – but are not the answer to the restlessness of the human condition? And, reflecting further on Jesus' self-identification as the Son of Man who has nowhere to rest his head (Luke 9.58), we might note the evangelistic imperative to preach the gospel to new communities in response to the Great Commandment, because the limitations of any given community constrain the possibilities of the gospel's new and disturbing challenge to settled-ness. Yet the trajectory of the New Testament faces towards the restoration of humanity's relationship with God – the end to the homelessness begun at the Fall. As Murray Rae puts it, in his fascinating study of architecture and theology, 'Now, in the Johannine literature, reconciliation with God comes about through the provision of a new dwelling place – in Christ and in his teaching.'[4]

Theology, Place . . . and Parish

In his ground-breaking approach to a theology of place, John Inge, Bishop of Worcester, notes that modernity set out to control and regiment the idea of place and ended up losing any worthwhile sense of place altogether.[5] He quotes Oliver O'Donovan's observation that 'local roots and rootlessness should be, one would think, a major topic of conversation among theologians who habitually read the Bible' – but observes that this is not the case. Both O'Donovan and Inge suggest that Protestant theology broke down 'elective particularity', not only of race (as the New Covenant extended beyond the people of Israel to all humanity) but also of place. One response, they suggest, is to reconnect with the idea of holy places. Inge goes on to develop a theology of sacramental places – places where intimations of God can be exceptionally clear. While many traditions within Christianity have tended to resist the idea of there being especially sacred spaces, the idea is certainly present in Celtic Christianity, which has had something of a revival in recent decades. The reason for this is perhaps, as many have suggested, because a facet of the new environmental awareness that seeks a reintegration of human life with the natural environment is in reaction to people's estrangement from their context that was one of the hallmarks of modernity's desire to control and dominate. Allied to the idea of sacred places is the notion of pilgrimage – places become sites to be sought out in search of spiritual experience. So a theology of the sacred may help us reconnect place to the search for God in the natural environment – but what of the contribution that the built environment might play in this? Sacred places may be marked by specific buildings – great cathedrals are an example. But modern-day notions of pilgrimage are not confined to the overtly sacred buildings of religious traditions, encompassing the terraced houses once inhabited by the Beatles, sites of great crimes or sudden deaths, or any location touched by notoriety or celebrity. Buildings may acquire meanings which verge on, or even become, the sacred, by associations of all kinds.

Inge argues that a renewed appreciation of the importance of place is one thing that Christian theology can offer to a world and culture that is characterized by the dislocation of human lives. The way we build houses can, potentially, contribute to, or hinder, this offering.

The Bible has more to say about the significance of place and people's relationship to place – perhaps a key text here is the story of Naboth's vineyard (1 Kings 21). Ahab the king desires the vineyard owned by Naboth and offers to buy it or to provide Naboth with a better one. But Naboth's response takes no account of this essentially commercial proposition. 'The Lord forbid that I should give you my ancestral inheritance' (1 Kings 21.3). Ahab's wife Jezebel has Naboth killed, and when Ahab takes possession of the vineyard both he and Jezebel are hotly condemned by Elijah – clearly the Lord's sympathies are all with Naboth. In Bible study sessions on that passage, the significance of place is often foremost in people's reflections on the text. It often becomes clear how strongly contemporary Western people empathize with the idea of ancestral inheritance determining the way in which people and places belong together, and this is not primarily a reflection on material ownership but on the way people identify with certain places and are distressed by being torn away from them – many will tell stories from their own experience which show how superficial our culture's conviction is that land ownership can be simply a matter for the market. People often feel that not only may they share in the ownership of the land or a specific place, but that deep within them is the sense that the land – the place – owns them. It is a mutual relationship of trust and stewardship that runs much deeper than legal or financial conventions.

While Inge tends to see a need for theology to focus once again on the significance of place, the particular inheritance of the Church of England is absolutely focused on place. To give a potted (and slightly tongue in cheek) account of the emergence of Anglicanism under Elizabeth I, and its consolidation with the later seventeenth-century divines, it is reasonable to understand the Church of England as being defined not by doctrine or leadership (as for 'Baptists' or 'Lutherans'), but by geography. For a country wearied by the religious warfare, persecutions and burnings of the Reformation, yet still divided between the more-Catholic and more-Protestant strands of the faith, the need for a settlement to put an end to the bloodshed made the nation the defining entity and the parish its local manifestation. The tensions between Catholics and Protestants had not gone away. There was no final synthesis of beliefs. Instead, building on the emergence of the nation-state as a primary unit of government and identity (itself both a symptom and a cause of the Reformation), the Church of England moved from being simply an administrative unit of the (Roman) Catholic ecclesial empire and made the geographical boundary of the nation, and national identity, fundamental to Christian conduct. You may have continued to believe your neighbour to be a wicked Papist (or Protestant) heretic, but now, united in Englishness, you were asked to worship alongside him in the parish church, with the monarch as Supreme Governor and only the more extreme forms of dissent (which could not accommodate compromise) outlawed. So a national Church expressed itself most authentically in the parish, which made geographical community and worshipping community effectively coterminous. So long as English people continued to identify strongly with place, this worked extraordinarily well.

It may, therefore, be no surprise that the erosion of a sense of place in the late phases of modernity has tested the parish system acutely. A mobile population discovered again that religion could be more congenial when you practised it alongside those who shared your doctrinal emphases. For years, it has been argued by some that 'postmodern people have no allegiance to place' and that the parish system should therefore give way to 'a networked church'. Pressed on what would constitute the warp and weft of the network, it usually reverts to money and doctrine – 'our' money must flow only to Christians who share 'our' precise beliefs and worship practices. Leaving aside the questionable notion of postmodernity here, which in fact is more characteristic of late-modernity, this is one facet of the erosion of an Anglican theology of place. It diminishes the theological significance of a framework within which different strands of the Christian tradition could correct and complement each other and where excessive certainty about God could be moderated by the equally excessive certainties of one's neighbour.[6]

Yet the Church of England continues to benefit greatly from its parish structure. Alone among the denominations, it remains 'a Christian presence in every community', allowing urban, rural and suburban communities, north and south, rich and poor, to each take their place in the journey of shared discipleship. That 'coverage', parish by parish, helps locate the Church of England in the minds of even its 'cultured despisers', and many who have no real belief in the God of Jesus Christ retain an affection for the Church of England seemingly bound up with a sense that the fragmentation of our times needs at least some institutional resistance to challenge the tired assumption that economic growth and wider education inevitably lead to secularization.

Recent years have seen a resurgence of theological exploration of the virtues and opportunities that the parish system affords. Andrew Rumsey's recent book, *Parish*, is a good example.[7] As he says, 'Parish is the nearby community: its vocation is to proximity . . . The biblical command to love our neighbour – literally, the one who is near or "nigh" – invests social proximity with divine potential' (p. 122). Long before Lloyd George implemented the first tentative steps towards a welfare state, the Anglican parish was the main vehicle (however inadequately it adjusted to social change) for the care of both the indigenous poor and needy and the vagrant 'other'. Importantly, Rumsey goes on to note the persistence of the parish ideal, not least as a basis for the persistence of religion which is so perplexing to confirmed secularists. He quotes the sociologist/theologian Timothy Jenkins's comment that the kind of communities he studied, whether inner urban or rural, 'were supposed to have disappeared . . . [but] have long existed behind the appearance of "being about to disappear"'. And, from the work of Malcolm Torry who has worked almost exclusively in inner urban parishes marked by radical change, such as the Greenwich Peninsula, 'The parish, understood as a patch of ground, as the people who live and work on it . . . has been and still is a bulwark against secularization in ways that other styles of religious organization cannot be.'

Whatever happens in response to the housing crisis will be played out in parishes – in England, there is no alternative. But as heirs of this peculiarly Anglican inheritance, how might we think about housing in ways that not only promote and sustain that rather nebulous concept of 'community', but which also promote flourishing parishes that can continue to contribute so much to the common good, not only of the faithful but of all people?

Constructing Community

The political philosopher Raymond Plant commented back in the 1970s that the word 'community' was extraordinarily hard to pin down to any substantive meaning.[8] It almost always signifies a concept that is approved of by the speaker, and sometimes the word is used unashamedly to imply collective virtue. But the complexities of human relationships, from the individual, through the family, to the nation and the world population (not forgetting intergenerational and historical linkages) renders the concept of community so multi-faceted and overlapping that it can mean everything and nothing. In normal parlance, community is usually found somewhere in the space between the family and the nation – although that gap is broad and complex enough.

It is interesting to see the shifting emphasis on community in some theological works between the 1960s and 1980s. In the 1960s, Harvey Cox's *The Secular City* celebrated the anonymity of the city as a major step forward from the oppressiveness of 'tradition' in many rural communities where one's identity was always constrained by one's family history.[9] The city, in contrast, offered the image and the reality of choice, self-realization and freedom. Only 20 years later, the report of the Archbishops' Commission on Urban Priority Areas (*Faith in the City*)[10] highlighted the deleterious loss of community bonds in inner-city areas (although it also noted their surprising resilience) and sought ways to rebuild structures of neighbourliness in the context of economic hardship. Also in the 1980s, following the publication of MacIntyre's *After Virtue*, a strong new interest emerged around the significance of tradition, narrative and community, as antidotes to the emerging weakness of Enlightenment Liberalism. Modernity's characteristic individualism, and various communitarian reactions against it, are characteristic of today's tensions in politics, philosophy, and disciplines as far removed from each other as theology and management theory.[11]

It is therefore important not to romanticize community but to seek ways to sustain the interesting tension between the autonomy of the individual, the centrality of the family (not least, in making real our inherent dependency on others) and wider community relationships of many kinds. The way housing is built – for example, 'defensive' or more open architecture – and arranged (long uniform terraces, courtyards, uniformity or variety of design) can clearly be instrumental in encouraging or frustrating these delicate balances.

After all, we now know a great deal about the effect of slum clearances in the 1950s and 1960s on the wellbeing of the people who were moved to fine new social housing, often a long bus ride from where they had grown into a community together. On the face of it, the new housing was a splendid improvement on what had gone before – and people were duly appreciative of the material gains they enjoyed. But it was in the non-material – the spiritual – dimension that their needs had been ignored, perhaps because the language of spiritual need was, and is, so hard to articulate. Depression, isolation and a sense of having lost a shared purpose became the story that accompanied the other narrative of sanitary, relatively spacious and modern housing.[12] And as these estates grew to maturity, in a new ideological environment that no longer saw social housing as a positive gain on what preceded it, but as an inferior option for people with no economic clout, the isolation from services, community solidarities and the wider world grew deeper. Lynsey Hanley writes eloquently of growing up on a Birmingham social housing estate, with 'a wall in my head'. Even though there were no physical barriers to leaving the estate and entering other spaces, the 'wall in the head' made it very clear that such other areas were 'not for people like us'. However necessary the slum replacement programmes had been, and however great the physical improvement in the housing, the dislocation of people from community, and the paradoxical creation of new 'communities' isolated from a richer sense of neighbourhood by their own self-perceptions, have been among those unexpected consequences of seeking the common good with too thin a sense of what thriving communities actually look like.[13]

As another check on nostalgic constructions of community, Gorringe notes that, for Aristotle, the city, not the village, was the quintessential community. There is something important here about scale. Aristotle's *civitas* was not today's London, Paris or Mumbai – it amounted to some 5,000 heads of households and about 35,000–40,000 people in all. But there is also an important point about the tension noted earlier between Cox's *Secular City* and the desire to rebuild small-scale community as an antidote to isolation. Despite the virtues of the village, its limitations are real. Despite the opportunities of the city, its inability to reflect the human scale is also a limitation. Could it be that people need to belong, at some level, to both the village and the city? To experience intimate belonging and to encounter the unexpected other fairly regularly? Something of this duality was captured in Ebenezer Howard's vision for the garden city that he created at Letchworth – attempting to bring together the 'town magnet' and the 'country magnet' so that each attracted the other. Gorringe is not afraid to speak of the garden city as attempting to embrace a theological idea.

Theology and the Built Environment

As Gorringe notes, 'Wittingly or unwittingly every design for council estates, every barrio, every skyscraper, every out of town supermarket, expresses a view of the human, embodies an ethic . . . ethics is the conversation of the human race about its common project.' He immediately aligns this insight with the Deuteronomic call for the people to choose between the way of life and the way of death. And he quotes Nicholas Wolterstorff's insight that true *shalom* means much more than 'a pietistic-materialistic understanding of man, viewing human needs as the need for a saved soul plus the need for food, clothes and shelter'. Like Wolterstorff, he stresses the need for the built environment to include edifices that people can delight in.

In discussing houses, Gorringe observes that, even in Neolithic times, the house was always more than a shelter: 'The centre of "secular" life was also the site of the sacred.' He goes on to discuss the way in which the focal point of our dwellings can express this sacred nature, and speaks of the 'altar corner' that epitomizes the function of the house in expressing something deeper than mere function. So, for the Victorians, the hearth was the site of the sacred (if, as Gorringe comments, Dickens is to be believed . . .) and sometimes it is the kitchen table. But he also notes how these focal points have been degraded or lost – the habit of 'snacking' takes away the sacred significance of the shared table; the prevalence of central heating leaves rooms unfocused with no heart. The 'altar corner' for many modern homes becomes, by default, the TV screen through which the occupants gaze into another reality, their faces turned away from one another towards the flickering image.

Housing Utopias and Self-help

The development of housing in Britain has sometimes been almost anarchic, sometimes planned; sometimes with a light touch and sometimes heavy-handedly. But there have also been self-conscious (in the best sense) attempts to develop housing in ways that encourage flourishing communities. There has often been a distinctly utopian element in these projects and a religious (often Christian) approach has sometimes underlain the experiment.

One example is the Bournville estate in Birmingham, developed by the Quaker George Cadbury at the end of the nineteenth century – not, as sometimes assumed, as housing for his company's workers (although some factory-related housing had been built on the site) but as an experimental model settlement. Bournville eventually comprised some 7,800 dwellings, set out with plenty of open spaces, shopping areas and leisure and community facilities, all administered since 1900 by the Bournville Village Trust. In 2003 Bournville was identified by the Joseph Rowntree Foundation (note the Quaker and chocolate connections!) as 'one of the nicest places to live in Britain', suggesting that the experiment had continued to succeed through the changes of over a century.

In contrast, the Bostall Estate in Abbey Wood, southeast London, was built in 1900–30 by the Royal Arsenal Co-operative Society. Following the tenets of the nonconformism that underlay the co-operative movement, the estate had some (Co-op) shops and one or two nonconformist places of worship, but no pubs or Anglican (or Catholic!) churches. The lack of pubs was felt keenly by the residents (mostly manual workers from Woolwich Arsenal). More recently, as pubs in the wider neighbourhood, and the small shops, Co-ops and Free Churches have declined and often closed, the estate feels something of a desert, with no easy access to essential services. In J. B. Priestley's phrase, which he applied to areas of bleak industrial housing, it may be a place to exist and work, but not a place to live.[14]

Both these examples (and there are many more, each with a unique story) suggest that the influence of an underlying theological rationale may help shape practical housing outcomes. Perhaps the difference between these two cases is that, at Bournville, the wealth of the Cadburys allowed a vision to be realized on generous grounds, whereas at Abbey Wood the religious vision of a community marked by temperance and piety had to rely on much thinner investment and a tighter balance sheet, exacerbated, perhaps, by London land prices.

Those examples show how a vision rooted in the Christian theology of an individual or small group might lead to housing and community outcomes enjoyed (or suffered) by many. It would be interesting to look more closely at the practices of religious groups like the Amish in Pennsylvania, or Mennonite communities, where a very strongly sectarian theology means that whole communities are created not only to embody religious principles, but as the collective effort of the community who will inhabit the place. The strong community ethos of the Amish comes across very clearly in the celebrated 'barn raising' sequence in the 1985 film *Witness* with Harrison Ford. It is fair to say that the general impression of most religiously inspired sectarian communities is more about coercion and the potential abuse of power than happy self-determination. But examples where religion and community are essentially coterminous and lead to workable models of housing and community building are still worth remembering.

Self-help, as a principle behind housing developments, has led to some interesting developments – with or without religious inspiration. In a book castigating the architectural awfulness that he dubs 'pseudo-modernism', Owen Hatherley (who is romantic about genuine postmodern or modernist architecture rather than retro kitsch) contrasts two recent housing developments in the post-industrial urban village of Ancoats in East Manchester. One, re-branded around the turn of the millennium as 'New Islington', replaced low-rise council housing with 'one (apparently hard to sell) Allsop block, two small closes of houses and a whole lot of verbiage'. Another, in the same area, 'presents more actual ideas than all the other recent buildings in the city put together'. Hatherley explains how this second development 'was an attempt to meet the tenants' own desires – for houses with gardens and decoration – without patronizing them'. The residents had chosen the developers, 'precisely because they seemed most interested in their own ideas, rather than slotting them into slick towers and their attendant loft-living lifestyle'.[15] Gorringe cites other studies of resident or tenant involvement in design issues, commenting that one difference between municipal estates and some sub-urban developments is not the quality of the building but the fact that, in the creation of one the people had some involvement and in the other they did not. Leaving aside Hatherley's idiosyncratic architectural judgements, there is something important here about how housing might be conceived, developed and built that is picked up later in this chapter in the concept of Subsidiarity.

It may be worth, however, entering one possible caveat to the inspiring principle that thorough consultation with tenants is the key to viable housing that builds genuine community – the fact that any house worthy of the name will outlive the generation that was involved in its planning. In Bournville, the initial vision has survived – equally appreciated it seems – for several generations. But that was one person's vision, not the result of collective consultation. We may need to ask if there are any long-standing examples of resident consultation where the judgement of the original cohort has proved robust and resilient through changing needs and contexts. Such consultation must, perforce, go deeper than transient questions of superficial appearance and décor. The theological point here is precisely the one with which this chapter opened – the essential ambiguity of permanent housing in a fallen world marked by change and conditionality, and the need for houses to be adaptable for the very different sort of restless nomadic lives that many live today.

A somewhat different example of self-help in housing – or rather, in the creation of community – comes in Rex Walford's magisterial study of the response by the churches to the growth of the north London suburbs between the wars.[16] Another study of suburban London, by Jackson, notes that most of the developments were speculative estates by building companies with variable levels of professional skill.[17] Some houses, though still standing today, were distinctly jerry-built – others less so. But whereas Jackson's view of the community life that grew up in these semi-detached suburbs is a caricature of individualistic, competitive (keeping up with the Jones's), secular and shallow suburban life, Walford (who lays a lot of blame for that caricature on Malcolm Muggeridge's book *The Thirties*) goes deeper to show how immense was the contribution of the Christian churches to the transition from new-build wasteland to thriving community life. Contrary to the Muggeridge/Jackson assertion that the iconic buildings of the 1930s were cinemas, Walford shows how many splendid suburban churches emerged in the

1930s – often funded and even part-built by their congregations who had made do for years with a tin-tabernacle, pre-fab hall or even a tent for worship. (It was not uncommon for the men of the congregation to dig the foundations themselves before the building contractors moved in – no doubt sustained by copious cups of tea from the women of the congregation … This certainly happened in my home parish south of the river.) But, more to our point, he also plots the extraordinarily rapid emergence of a plethora of parish-based voluntary groups as new residents arriving either from the old inner-city areas or from more rural backgrounds, shook down into something resembling a real community. Within a very short time of the first residents moving in (often one to two years), there were uniformed youth organizations, Mothers' Unions, Working Men's Clubs, Gardening and Amateur Dramatic Societies, choirs, and many more. Walford notes with regret that it is impossible to quantify the number of individuals involved (the Cub Mistress may also have been a leading light in the Gardening Club) but it was clearly considerable. My own research suggested that these community-forming church-based groups largely survived until the early 1970s and then died rapidly – most probably as the last of the original inhabitants of the estate died out.[18] It is possible that the failure to hand on this model of organization-based community-building to subsequent generations indicated that they were, to some extent, palliative measures compensating for the loss of a more indigenous kind of community remembered fondly from the Bermondsey tenements or Middlesex villages – but many other factors, which have made the second half of the twentieth century and beyond so individualistic and secular, would have to be factored in too. Nonetheless, as a model for establishing thriving churches in apparently god-less new housing areas, the 1930s approach may persist in some of the new housing areas of the twenty-first century where a small Christian congregation, often starting by using a school hall as a temporary place of worship, focuses on structures and voluntary activities that bring otherwise-estranged people together.

Is There a Christian Architecture?

According to David Watkin, 'The central argument of Pugin's *Contrasts* (1836) is that there is a necessary connection between religious truth and architectural truth.'[19] Indeed, the burden of Watkin's book is an attempt to debunk this idea and its subsequent (post-Christian) variants. Pugin, a Catholic convert, noted the rise of neo-Classical architecture, which he deplored, at roughly the time of the Reformation, which he also deplored, and so assumed a causal relationship between the two. Pugin argued that people could live better if surrounded by Gothic, rather than Classical, architectural detail, and illustrated this in his later book, *An Apology for the Revival of Christian Architecture in England* (1843), with tendentious pictures of the two styles in modern settings. In Pugin's pictures of railway stations, 'Even the trains seem to respond to the "improved" architecture: while the engine at (Classical) Euston disfigures the station with clouds of smoke and steam, an engine in the Gothic station allows itself no more than a few Picturesque puffs.'[20] One of Pugin's unrealized ambitions was to produce a treatise on Natural Architecture in a kind of parallel of Natural Theology, in which the existence and nature of God can be inferred from the created order. For him, the Gothic style embodied theological truth. Watkin reasonably describes Pugin's argument – that the right sort of architecture can be seen to convey unchanging theological truth – as a heresy, and comments that had the Vatican read his books (or cared enough about them) Pugin would have been excommunicated.

But Watkin makes a much more serious point in chastising Pugin: he argues that later architectural apologias have followed Pugin in attributing to architecture the power to convey not just religious truth, but also ideological truth. Thus, le Corbusier is quoted extensively to show how he understood his designs to be promoting a better form of human existence. Le Corbusier's celebrated maxim that a house is 'a machine for living in' – one that is 'healthy (and morally so too)' – aligns with his belief that architecture conveys truth – a specific form of truth to be sure – and must be challenged if it attempts to convey any kind of truth with which le Corbusier disagrees. For this school of design, the truth that the right sort of architecture conveys is the truth of the revolution, the break with old social orders and the opening of a new era of ordered, machine-like, human society.

Watkin goes on to detect a similar kind of heresy in many other architectural schools. His book is entertaining and insightful in the best Peterhouse High Tory tradition in which he stood – but is he right? The way he draws parallels between Pugin's Catholic interests and le Corbusier's Marxist ones should at least give us pause for thought. If we approach the built environment – including housing – in the belief that, done well, it can help communities to flourish, can we be sure that we are not imposing on this argument our own (perhaps more biased than we realize) perceptions of what a flourishing community must be like? It is, at the very least, a warning not to believe that God has sanctioned any specific form of building or edifice. The truth of the gospel may be obscured by all manner of human creations – tawdry buildings presented as the last word, ramshackle housing fobbed off on the poor, estates built to deliberately frustrate human interaction – but no one approach uniquely encapsulates gospel truth.

But if we expand our horizon beyond the narrow discipline of architecture, there may be more to say about Christian approaches to building – including the building of houses. Gorringe, whose work on theology and the built environment reflects also his long-standing concern for theology and the environment, points out that buildings account for 46 per cent of carbon dioxide emissions (and, when construction is added in, over 50 per cent).[21] How we design and build, including our houses, reflects the care we take, or do not take, of God's whole created order.

This leads us inexorably towards the important theological concept of the Common Good. Although the concept of the Common Good has long been familiar in Anglicanism (for instance, in the prayers of intercession in the *ASB* and *Common Worship*) its origins in Catholic Social Teaching go much deeper. In Catholic Social Teaching, the Common Good is held in tension with, and is balanced by, the principle of Subsidiarity. The Common Good principle urges us to focus on what we share as people and how our personal welfare is bound up with that of our fellow human beings so that our flourishing tends to be maximized when the overall flourishing of all people is attended to. Subsidiarity is not in contradiction with that principle but stresses that decisions and actions ought to take place at the lowest level consistent with effectiveness. Thus, decisions about priorities in local government, aimed at the common good of the local community, ought not to be taken by national government or large, non-local, corporations. If such decisions can effectively be taken and implemented by local people themselves, that is where they should be settled.

A Very Tentative Conclusion

The more one considers housing, the more interdependent the subject becomes, asking wider questions – hence the emphasis here on place, community, utopias and real examples. Exploring what is possible in terms of housing could be a comparatively simple exercise in cost-effectiveness and political possibility, informed by a superficially incarnational theology that so strongly identifies the presence of Christ among us with a divine endorsement of the material world that the Fall and its consequences are obscured and a Christ-like concern for the needy totally fills the lens through which we approach the questions.

But, as Nicholas Lash has pointed out, the classic Christian grammar locates our lives simultaneously on both sides of the cross. To be sure, we inhabit a world in which resurrection is a known truth and the Pentecost gift of the Spirit a reality. But it remains a world marked by the persistence of sin, in which we continue to await the second coming of Christ when the kingdom now inaugurated will be completed under God.

Living on both sides of the cross, our attempts to live as disciples are always likely to be paradoxical – our best intentions and actions having unforeseen consequences, and God's hand emerging in strange and disturbing ways in actions we never expected to be vehicles for the divine. We have noted the paradox of being a spiritually nomadic people, open to the call to up-sticks and follow a strange vocation, while still craving (and needing) stability, predictability and – most of all – other people surrounding us as neighbours and not just as random others. There is the paradox that community is simultaneously liberating and constraining – and the paradox that there are many communities whose often conflicting needs and aspirations cannot all be met in a finite world, but where community life is often the vehicle through which we can break out from the limitations that seem to surround us. And there is the paradox that the kinds of community we are most easily able to envisage often leave out the stresses, conflicts and tensions that actually make good community possible.

As a people whose faith is grounded in the extraordinary paradoxes that accompany God's interventions in the world – especially the paradox surrounding God's own Son who comes among us, not just as human but as one with nowhere to lay his head – Christians ought to be able to work well with paradox. And, if we are Anglicans, we have some important ecclesiological assets – especially the parish – around which a creative, effective and ultimate human approach to housing could emerge.

Notes

1 MacIntyre, A. (1999), *Dependent, Rational Animals*, London: Duckworth, 1999.

2 Priestley, J. B. (2018), *English Journey*, Bradford: Great Northern Books Ltd (orig. 1933) is eloquent on this topic.

3 A well-known book by the American ethicist Stanley Hauerwas picks up this phrase as its title and offers a helpful exploration of the ethical implications of the Christian ambiguity about permanence and community. Hauerwas, S. and Willimon, W. H. (1989), *Resident Aliens: Life in the Christian Colony*, Nashville, TN: Abingdon Press.

4 Rae, M. (2017), *Architecture and Theology: The Art of Place*, Waco, TX: Baylor University Press.

5 Inge, J. (2003), *A Christian Theology of Place*, Aldershot: Ashgate Press, p. 28.

6 For a discursive account of how the Anglican tradition has understood the social aspect of its theology, see Brown, M., ed. (2014), *Anglican Social Theology*, London: Church House Publishing.

7 Rumsey, A. (2017), *Parish: An Anglican Theology of Place*, London: SCM Press.

8 Plant, R. (1978), 'Community: Concept, Conception and Ideology', *Politics and Society*, vol. 8, no. 1, pp. 79–107.

9 Cox, H. (1965), *The Secular City*, London: SCM Press.

10 ACUPA (1985), *Faith in the City*, London: Church House Publishing, 1985.

11 MacIntyre, A. (1985), *After Virtue: A Study in Moral Theory*, 2nd edn, London: Duckworth. Articles explicitly exploring MacIntyre's arguments have appeared in journals on management, architecture and many other disciplines. The search for a new politics of community is at the heart of the political movements known as 'Red Tory' and 'Blue Labour' and had a tentative outing in Theresa May's 2017 manifesto (only to take the blame, probably unjustly, for her electoral failure). The tension between liberalism and communitarianism is explored in depth in Brown, M. (2010), *Tensions in Christian Ethics*, London: SPCK.

12 Hoggart, R. (2007), *The Uses of Literacy*, Harmondsworth: Penguin, p. 19.

13 Hanley, L. (2007), *Estates: An Intimate History*, London: Granta Books.

14 Priestley, *English Journey*.

15 Hatherley, O. (2010), *A Guide to the New Ruins of Great Britain*, London: Verso.

16 Walford, R. (2007), *The Growth of 'New London' in Suburban Middlesex (1918–1945) and the Response of the Church of England*, Lampeter: Edwin Mellen Press.

17 Jackson, A. A. (1991), *Semi-Detached London*, 2nd edn, Didcot: Wild Swan.

18 Brown, M. (2005), *Faith in Suburbia: Completing the Contextual Trilogy*, Contact Pastoral Monographs, no. 15.

19 Watkin, D. (1977), *Morality and Architecture*, Oxford: Clarendon Press.

20 Watkin, *Morality*, p. 22.

21 Gorringe, T. J. (2002), *A Theology of the Built Environment: Justice, Empowerment, Redemption*, Cambridge: Cambridge University Press, p. 224.

5

Generation, Degeneration, Regeneration: The Theological Architecture and Horticulture of a Deprived Housing Estate

SAMUEL WELLS

Around the turn of the millennium I experienced the biggest theological challenge I've faced in ministry. In 1996 I applied to be the vicar of a small church on a housing estate in Norwich. Norwich was England's second city in the seventeenth century, when the wealth of the wool trade brought it a church for every week of the year and a pub for every day. But the church where I was seeking to become vicar was rather different. Its membership numbered around 25 and the neighbourhood it served was the most materially disadvantaged in the east of England. I was excited to be invited to meet the bishop to discuss the position. I later discovered I was the only applicant for the job. The bishop said to me, with disarming frankness, 'Why does a person with a PhD want a job like this?' I replied, 'Because I want to see Jesus and to discover the kingdom of God.'

I grew up in the Church at a time when being radical was easy. Prime Minister Margaret Thatcher was embarking on a series of austerity measures that reduced investment in welfare and public services. There were riots in major cities, and the Church of England's *Faith in the City* report was critical of the government's neglect of the urban poor. And then Mrs Thatcher defined the era by making her most notorious remark, 'There is no such thing as society.' You could think yourself radical just by being against Mrs Thatcher.

But by the time I moved to Norwich 15 years later there was a new government and a new philosophy. In 1998 Tony Blair announced that 17 socially disadvantaged areas would be identified and £35 million would be made available to each one if its local residents could organize themselves into a board and committees to run their own regeneration. It turned out my neighbourhood was identified as one of the 17. So I found myself taking on a new unpaid additional job as a community organizer and helping to lead a mass democratic regeneration movement for the next five years. We eventually formed the first development trust in the Eastern region, and set about doing community surveys and elections and generally poking our fingers into everything.

And this was the moment when I felt overwhelmed by the biggest theological challenge I've had in ministry. Imagine you're faced with a significant level of social deprivation, and you have pretty much all the money you could dream of to do something about it. You can't blame the government, because they've given you all the help you could ask for. What do you do? Put another way, here is an underclass neighbourhood. It's widely seen around the city and region as a dangerous place that's a drain on more comfortable suburbs and hard-working taxpayers and productive businesses. What would redemption look like for such a community? Should you strive to make it look as much like one of the more affluent middle-class suburbs as possible? Is it distinctive only for what it's not, or is there an elixir of life at the heart of the neighbourhood around which can cluster a whole host of initiatives and green shoots of regeneration?

I struggled with that question all through those years – and I've struggled with it ever since. I went to live in the neighbourhood and I got involved in the regeneration process because I wanted to be with people in their sorrows and struggles, and find beauty and abundance where some might only see shame and scarcity. But then I had to allow my imagination to be stretched to a vision of what it might mean for this community genuinely to flourish, to be happy and settled and at peace with itself. And that was somehow harder. The process of regeneration exposes deep assumptions in all parties involved: it reveals significant, and sometimes contradictory, notions of human flourishing; and it evokes rival perceptions of the cause and character of constraints on human wellbeing. I concentrate on the theological notions of generation and degeneration, or creation and fall, because it is these perceptions, of how things were intended to be and in what respects they have gone wrong, that tend to shape consequent assumptions about the need, goal, and methods of regeneration.

The status of a deprived housing estate before God is in principle no different to the status of the rest of God's creation. It is good, but fallen. It is waiting with eager longing for glorious liberty under God.

The designation of a housing estate as 'good' means a number of things theologically. It means that God meant it to be so. It has within it the seeds of its own flourishing. 'Good' does not mean 'perfect'. But it does mean that God says to the estate and its residents, 'I made you this way because I wanted one like you.' The assumption behind a great deal of what is called regeneration is that the estate in question is not good – and often that the people who live on it are not good either. 'Regeneration' is a theological term that refers to rebirth, or the restoration of a time before fallenness. Thus to be publicly regarded as suitable for regeneration, a community or individual must be one whose mortality or depravity particularly stands out. To qualify for large government grants, it is necessary to parade a desultory display of ugly statistics. An estate has to gain attention as a miserable sinner before it can qualify to be saved – however demeaning this process of attention-seeking may be.

In the language used about a housing estate, the tendency is to concentrate on what an outsider perceives it lacks, rather than on what an insider perceives it has. 'Deprived' suggests an estate is entitled to something but that thing has been taken away from it. 'Disadvantaged' suggests that other communities have a head start, whereas this estate has, through no fault of its own, some kind of a handicap. 'Priority', 'challenging' or 'tough' tend to be words of professional outsiders, reflecting on their perceptions of the intractable problems of the community; meanwhile, other outsiders tend to use more direct language such as 'rough', or even 'bad'. If these negative perceptions of outsiders are the only words that are ever used to characterize the estate, the community will always be dominated by the shame of what it is not, rather than the pride of what it is. The day when those who sought partners of the same sex began to choose the designation 'gay' was a highly significant moment in transforming attitudes to sexuality. A housing estate seeking to make the most of the opportunities available for its own development may similarly need to coin its own designation.

Assessing the redemption of the fallen world, two theological principles seem to be in conflict. On the one hand, God is transcendent, totally other than the creation, and in entire authority over it. Thus the best human efforts pale compared with the glory of God. On the other hand, the Trinity is committed to the creation it has made, however flawed its current state. After the Flood, God promised Noah that the creation would never again be destroyed. This initiated the task of redeeming, rather than rejecting, even the most challenging aspects of what had been made. Thus, in the words of Thomas Aquinas, 'grace does not destroy, but presupposes and perfects nature'; in the words of Jürgen Moltmann, 'grace . . . prepares nature for eternal glory'. In other words, any lasting regeneration must be built on the positive aspects of the culture that already exists. The first theological question about a deprived estate is, how does God see this estate? Is what deprived estates have in common (relative economic poverty) the first thing God sees, or does the divine gaze principally fall on their unique, diverse, and perhaps more positive aspects?

The notion of God's good creation implies a richer description of 'good'. 'Good' means that creatures are interdependent, as well as dependent on God; that human beings are created for free and glad relationship in the image of God; and that God's creative purpose seeks ultimate fulfilment. If an estate is to be described in theological language as deprived, it must be because it is impoverished in one or more of these areas: dependence, relationship and fulfilment.

Immediately the language of deprivation seems inadequate. No one is deprived of the gracious love of God. God's love is as freely available – and frequently as freely received – on a housing estate as anywhere else. Many on housing estates, as elsewhere, are indeed deprived of the experience and knowledge of God's love. And all have fallen short of God's ultimate purpose. But there is little or nothing here that marks a deprived housing estate out from wealthier places. The spontaneity of joy, the awed gasp of wonder, the tears of gratitude and reconciliation, the abiding habits of mutual love: wealthier places have no patent on these. Many residents on such estates know this, and thus seldom glance naively at wealthier places as if affluence brought happiness. So what does it mean to talk of deprivation?

The more significant aspects of deprivation lie in dependence and relationship. Traditional Christian theology differs here from contemporary ideology: for in the language of our day, dependence is always a bad thing. For Christians, by contrast, dependence itself is not wrong. Indeed, dependence is the right state of the human relationship with God. A person who is appropriately dependent on God can form a suitable interdependent pattern of relationships with other people and the whole creation. Dependence only becomes a problem when a person does not found their life on appropriate dependence on God, and instead becomes dependent on other things: things that are less than God, which Christians traditionally call idols. An idol on a housing estate can mean another *person* – such as a loan shark – or a *thing* – such as an addictive drug. When dependence means subjection to the wrong things, it is called oppression. Oppressive dependence invariably leads to relationships that are anything but the free and glad expressions intended for those who worship, and thus depend on, God. If estates are called 'deprived', then in theological terms this must mean that such significant numbers of residents are locked into an oppressive pattern of dependent relationships that one can perceive the condition of the community as a whole in the language of slavery. A slave is deprived of freedom. Thus the conventional language of deprivation and disadvantage, which is the language of equality, masks the real issue, which is one of liberty.

If estates are created, they are also fallen. The language of regeneration carries a deep optimism that the application of the right strategies with the appropriate degree of partnership and determination will bring constructive change to deprived neighbourhoods. This constructive change amounts to the restoration of freedom to those who find themselves enslaved by poverty. But the Christian understanding of fallen humanity perceives that, given the choice between freedom and slavery, we human beings frequently choose slavery; that we humans invariably renounce grace and thankfulness; that we choose the idolatry of self or other; that we refuse to use our imagination to envisage the boundless possibilities of created life and the limitless destiny of everlasting life; that we opt instead for domination or servility. In the words of a Romanian woman on Boxing Day 1989, after the execution of President Ceauşescu, 'We have freedom, but we don't know what to do with it.' Some of the most interesting theological questions concerning urban regeneration arise from the notion of fallenness. What is perceived to be amiss? And whose fault is it?

If sin is largely about relationships, about the wrong form of dependence and resultant enslavement, then the sin in urban deprivation cannot lie simply within the estates themselves. All have sinned and fallen short of the grace of God. Areas become known as deprived because their indicators fall well below accepted norms. The language of regeneration implies that if only deprived communities could plateau out at the employment, education, health and crime levels of more affluent neighbourhoods, all would be well. But would it? This way of describing society unquestioningly accepts suburban values as the norm. If all have sinned, the poverty of the few is the responsibility of the many. It seems that there is something about the way society is structured that fosters the concentration of poverty in deprived areas.

The nature and location of sin are not the only points at

issue. Also in question is the unit by which humanity measures itself and is judged. Are we humans political animals, or are we accountable individuals? The more right-wing perception of poorer neighbourhoods as harbours for indigents is based on an individualist account of human being, and accordingly seeks a remedy in the rescue of individuals. The more left-wing perception of such communities as suffering from the structural sins of capitalist economics is based on a more corporate account of human identity, and seeks improvement by removing the structural obstacles to communal fulfilment. Both draw on the witness of Christ and the early Church for examples and inspiration.

The rival perceptions are reflected in the parallel understandings that residents and civil servants tend to have of sin and redemption. In the late 1990s and early 2000s I found that civil servants, carrying out New Labour policy, tended towards an Augustinian notion of salvation. That is, the presupposition was that a range of things were fundamentally wrong with the estate, including the attitudes and aspirations of many of the residents, and that these had to change if regeneration was to take place. Residents, at least those who gained a sense of general public support and thus authority, tended to see things rather differently. Adopting an Irenaean soteriology, they tended not to suppose that there was anything fundamentally wrong with the estate: rather, they tended to perceive the principal problem was that the estate was under-resourced, and that local people had too little say in how the scarce resources were assigned, so the resources that were indeed available were not appropriately distributed.

Rival Augustinian and Irenaean soteriologies have corresponding notions of heaven and hell, albeit realized ones. The underlying governmental eschatology was of a heaven based around equality of opportunity. This was a largely individualist heaven, where each person had the chance to live a life of autonomous choices, unencumbered by any disadvantages experienced in the culture of their upbringing. Meanwhile the lingering threat of hell was that government welfare, which was perceived as trapping people in poverty rather than acting as a safety net from poverty, or a helping hand out of poverty, would eventually be withdrawn from those who proved unable or unwilling to enter the heaven of autonomous lives. The Irenaean, or vocal residents', notion of hell was less developed. Heaven was a better-resourced version of the status quo, in which people could increase their self-respect by making an honest living out of activities that previously were limited to voluntary activity or the grey economy. The creeping suspicion was that the government's idea of heaven might be the vocal residents' idea of hell – that is, a society of educated, autonomous, mobile individuals who almost inevitably abandoned the more static, introverted, extended family structure of the estate.

There were two scapegoats that both parties could often be brought to agree on. One was the notion of problem families. When the most pressing issues seemed to be petty crime and unruly behaviour, the temptation was to identify the small number of households from which a large proportion of the disturbance seemed to come. Evicting those families was often a popular form of salvation, though of course it was not a solution. A second scapegoat was the living accommodation. Perhaps the most common symbol of regeneration is the demolition of failed housing schemes, each one a blighted utopia, and their replacement with new property. These two scapegoats raise significant theological questions. Are some aspects of human life beyond redemption? Are some practices and institutions of government beyond reform? Are problem families and inadequate housing distractions from addressing more fundamental issues? It is often said that dealing with buildings only deals with the surface of the problem – but less often said what the heart of the problem really is.

A helpful way of bringing these questions together is to explore two rival metaphors. On the one hand, regeneration may be seen as the work of a builder. Regeneration, as a building, must be on deep and reliable foundations: it takes collective effort; it looks perfect on the day it is completed; it requires constant maintenance. On the other hand, regeneration may be seen as the work of a gardener. As a garden, it takes time to grow; it cannot be rushed; it gets better the longer it lives; it requires constant weeding. The difference between them can be summarized in one sentence: that which is planted begins immediately to grow, while that which is built begins immediately to decay. Both metaphors find scriptural precedent. The language of garden is largely that of continuity: as Genesis begins in a garden and Revelation ends with a garden, so the new creation begins in John 20 with a man and a woman in a garden. The language of building is largely that of contrast: the central contrast is between the exclusive building, the temple, and the inclusive person, the Body of Christ.

The initiative with which I was for several years closely involved, the New Deal for Communities, emphasized that regeneration is about people rather than buildings. This suits the organic style of metaphor. But the traditional strength of the construction metaphor, as in phrases like 'building the new Jerusalem', is in its ability to provide physical, tangible results. Outcomes that involve people growing are notoriously difficult to measure. Meanwhile, the suggestion that people might, can or should grow implies a criticism that they themselves are not fully developed, and thus that the issue of poverty is about people themselves, not about circumstances, environment, or troublesome neighbours. The garden metaphor, though it seems to be about continuity, is in fact a more challenging one, since it accepts that it is people, rather than buildings, that need to change and grow. This challenge is less threatening when the emphasis is on redemption rather than fall. Regardless of the reasons for falling into poverty, it is local people, through their own growth, that carry the seeds of redemption.

For all the promise of the garden metaphor, and for all the temptation of the building metaphor, the underlying theological understanding at work in contemporary urban regeneration is neither of these: it is the metaphor of exile. Neglected urban areas are described as 'wastelands' and 'wildernesses', echoing the language of Isaiah, Jeremiah and Lamentations. Underclass estates are a 'problem' because they are islands of low economic activity, remarkably disengaged from the rest of society. In a culture increasingly characterized by a market that stretches across continents and even a planet, an estate that interacts relatively little with its city, let alone its region, is bound to seem a troublesome anomaly. The talents the residents could bring to the wider economy are largely hidden. Even more distressingly, wider society is maintaining and underwriting this alienation and isolation through the benefits system. How the exile came about is seldom discussed in detail. But the aspirations for return have much in common with the language of Isaiah 65: 'They shall build houses and inhabit them; they shall plant vineyards and eat their fruit . . . They shall not labour in vain, or bear children for calamity' (Isa. 65.21–23). The underlying language is that of returning home.

There remain two further assumptions about regeneration that need to be examined. The first is that regeneration – whether through changed hearts and minds or through reoriented resources – can work. Here we come to the tradition of original sin. Sin does not go away, just because people strive to overcome it. Its insidious character infects not just that which all recognize as evil but also that which all commend as good. The cause of regenerating deprived communities seems true to the upside-down kingdom of the Beatitudes. It enacts the promise that the meek will inherit the earth. But this provokes Kin Hubbard's reflection, 'I wonder how long the meek will keep the earth after they inherit it.' It is so easy for new regimes to replicate the oppressive behaviour of those they have replaced. Regeneration may alter the schedule of winners and losers. But can it make all winners? Those involved in ministry in such communities know that the choices and dilemmas of the gospel become sharply focused. It is not clear, for example, whether the Church's gospel is primarily about helping people recognize and come to terms with their limitations (through repentance and forgiveness) or about helping people unleash their limitless potential (through education and training). However much the Church applauds the sharing of opportunities among all manner and conditions of people, it at some stage has to remember that we are fallen creatures, not self-made angels. The Church is likely to have a role to play in regeneration programmes if it is recognized that it has consistently spoken the language of hope through perhaps lengthy periods of despair. It will continue to have a role to play, after the financial investment has gone, if it is able to recognize and face the almost inevitable reality of human weakness and sin without falling into disillusionment and cynicism.

The remaining assumption about creation concerns competition. Beneath the surface of regeneration strategies lie rival notions of human character and flourishing. The very process by which communities gain regeneration funding is often competitive. The notion of competition lay at the heart of twentieth-century political debates about capitalism and socialism. The one side said competition was indispensable and good, because quality floated to the top. The other side said competition was dispensable and bad, because quantity sank to the bottom. A widespread fear in cities that are committed to the regeneration of their poorer estates is that, as the health of one community begins to improve, the problems simply start to reappear elsewhere in the city. Is competition a good thing? Is the regeneration of one community inevitably at the expense of other communities, in this country or elsewhere? If every community in this country lifts itself out of poverty, will this lead to greater poverty in the developing world – or will the greater affluence in this country create more wealth to buy products made in the poorer South? The Church lives in a world where competition is commonplace – but it is not clear whether it believes competition is right or wrong, benevolent or demonic, inevitable or undesirable, a tool to be used or a force to be resisted.

I've asked a lot of questions. The reader may be feeling it's time for some answers. I might not be the right person to offer those answers. Some would say that role (largely or entirely) falls to those who continue to live on that estate, and others like it. Nonetheless as I reflect back 20 years later, here are some thoughts towards a resolution of some of these questions. Rather than offer something sweeping and comprehensive, I'm going to concentrate on the words of Isaiah 65, a key passage in understanding a scriptural vision of regeneration.

When the prophets of the Old Testament talked about regeneration and social hope they tended to do it in one of two ways.

One way, favoured by the book of Zechariah, was to long for political restoration, to put King David back on the throne and to have Israel king among the nations once again. The other way, portrayed by the book of Daniel, was to imagine a dramatic apocalyptic intervention of God that brought history to an end. You could call the first way 'earth' and the second way 'heaven'. Zechariah's way appealed to an activist spirit; the main drawback was that it was so much about Israel taking its destiny into its own hands that it didn't leave much room for faith in God's action. Daniel's way was all about God's action, but so much so that it encouraged a passive resignation among the people. Little has changed. Those who talk about salvation today tend to be either those who assume it comes from us so get off your backside, or those who assume it all comes from God – so you might as well stay on your backside.

And that's the context that explains why the vision of Isaiah 65 is so significant and so compelling. It's about God's action. It talks about 'new heavens and a new earth' – so it's obviously about the dramatic and decisive intervention of God. But its details are about children's wellbeing, people building houses, and growing crops – things as practical and mundane as a local councillor's electoral platform. What's breathtaking about the picture offered in Isaiah 65 is that it's poised between heaven and earth – poised between God's action and human action, poised between hope and pragmatism, poised between astonished wonder and hard-won realism, poised between the unknown future and the very ordinary present tense.

Looking a little more closely at the way Isaiah combines a vision of God and humanity, with each playing its full role in redemption, there are three dimensions to salvation in his description – three answers to my question back in Norwich, my question about what it made sense to hope for. The first is about health and wellbeing. 'No more shall there be . . . an infant that lives but a few days,' it says, 'or an old person who does not live out a lifetime' (Isa. 65.20). You always have to remember that in the Bible salvation and health are the same thing. Salvation means safety, and permanent relationship with God. Whenever we are anxious about our own health or the health of someone we love, we understand exactly how closely salvation and health are connected. We want salvation to make us better. Of course we do.

The second dimension is security – that when you build a house you get to live in it, and when you plant vineyards you get to enjoy their fruit. Two and a half thousand years before Karl Marx, Isaiah offers a manifesto for an alternative to slavery or indentured labour or oppressive social structures. Here is a picture of a happy, productive world where everyone gets to make and grow and enjoy and no one has to be exploited or used or alienated. Isaiah assumes it's good to work. This isn't a picture of angels playing harps. Work is at the heart of earth and heaven. There's no better feeling in life than to have good work to do, and to share in doing it with trusted and respected colleagues. Work is at the centre of how human beings turn earth into heaven and bring heaven to earth, blending the gifts of God with the labour of human hands. We only need to imagine being able to work knowing that our conditions of work would be fertile and all our labours would be fruitful. It's inspiring and energizing. It's a meeting of heaven and earth.

The third dimension is about the relationship to the soil, to food, and to animals. We are given this evocative picture: 'The wolf and the lamb shall feed together, the lion shall eat straw like the ox.' The message here is that the wider relationships that make human habitation possible are not fundamentally conflictual. Isaiah goes on, 'They shall not hurt or destroy on all my holy mountain, says the Lord.' This is the biggest philosophical claim in the whole of Isaiah's vision. It's the promise that when heaven and earth meet there isn't war, but partnership; not battle, but beauty; not a contest for scarce resources, but an act of worship centred on the sharing of food. A Eucharist, perhaps.

So this is Isaiah's answer to my long heartsearching about what to hope for in a disadvantaged neighbourhood. First, foster the right conditions for people's wellbeing. Salvation begins with health. Second, make possible constructive, rewarding and fruitful work. Thus may people discover the electric excitement of enjoying the work of their own hands. And

87

third, heal relationships, between people and one another, people and animals, and people and the soil.

That's a pretty comprehensive manifesto. It's not otherworldly and out of touch. But it's not so down to earth that it's easily within reach. It's poised between heaven and earth. But it's missing one thing that's laced through Isaiah's vision. When I was organizing on the housing estate in Norwich, I would often be bewildered that there was no place for faith in our conversations. We would have big meetings with huge challenges, but we would never start with a prayer. That meant we were simply relying on our own strength. We had squabbles about whose work was recognized in the media and celebrated in the community. But we had no way of talking about whose work most closely resembled God's kingdom. I found that work exhausting in a way I've never found church work exhausting, because we had no hands but our own to work with. But Isaiah infuses his vision with the presence of God. God is more intimately involved in redemption than the people themselves. God says, 'Before they call I will answer, while they are yet speaking I will hear' (Isa. 65.24). This is a thrilling description of God as one who knows our thoughts and our interests and our flourishing better than we do, but lets us enjoy the work of our hands anyway. Most wonderfully of all, God says, 'I am about to create Jerusalem as a joy, and its people as a delight. I will rejoice in Jerusalem, and delight in my people' (Isa. 65.18–19). Our lives are God's delight. This is the epitome of heaven – the discovery that God's life is shaped for our flourishing, that God's joy is us.

I look back 20 years and think, if I'd spent a little more time with Isaiah, I might have felt a clearer answer to my question. Bodily wellbeing, creative and fruitful labour, healthy interpersonal, political and environmental relationships: this really is a manifesto for any kind of people, however varied the realities or their economic or social circumstances. But now I see what I was struggling with wasn't fundamentally or specifically about poverty. It was about what we are each to hope for in this life, and what it means to strive for flourishing life in God's kingdom. I was trying to discover what it means to long for God's transformation, and yet take active small steps in the meantime to imitate the wellbeing, fruitfulness and harmony that only God can finally bring. In other words, what it means to be poised between heaven and earth.

The creation stories in Genesis were read by a people looking back over their history in the light of exodus from Egypt and exile in Babylon; the stories read by the early Christians, with a new experience of liberation in Christ and a new notion of exile from heaven. In both cases creation spoke of God's sovereignty and purpose, which was good news in times of trial. This chapter has sought to consider another notion of regeneration, that of community-led government investment, by again looking behind and beyond it to the perceptions of human flourishing and constraint on which it rests. A fuller study would reflect on the character of God, the way in which God loves and redeems the estates, the way the Church imitates God's love for these communities and seeks to model what their eschatological 'estate' looks like, and lastly the destiny of the estates. But I hope I have said enough to show that, while urban regeneration seems to be a rival model of redemption, and thus an idol, it can prove to be a stimulus to the Church's reflection on its own faith in God's purpose in creation, and thus a prophet.

(This is a revised and considerably expanded version of an article of the same title first published in *Political Theology*, 3/2 (2002), pp. 238–44.)

6

Building Together: Catholic and Pentecostal Perspectives on Theology and Housing

SHERMARA FLETCHER, ANGUS RITCHIE AND SELINA STONE

Introduction

A good starting-point for ecumenical engagement is to wonder 'How can we recognize one another as bearing distinctive gifts to build up the Body of Christ?' Such a question need not imply that our differences are insignificant. But it invites each of us to acknowledge the incompleteness of our witness to Christ; and to wonder what gifts others might bring to make that witness more faithful and effective.

None of the authors of this chapter was raised an Anglican. One of the features of the Church of England that has drawn each of us, in different ways, into its life is its commitment to place. The parochial system embodies a vision of Christian community in which the congregation has a commitment to the wellbeing of the wider parish in which it is set. This vision embraces a wide variety of contexts: from the Anglo-Saxon church, whose very walls tell the history of the rural village in which it is set, to the church on an inner-city estate that has remained 'present and engaged' when many other institutions have moved out of the neighbourhood.

This strength of Anglicanism is intertwined with one of its common weaknesses. As the Established Church, Anglican congregations have a tendency to view social issues such as housing from the perspective of the privileged and powerful more than that of ordinary citizens. As we shall argue in this chapter, Roman Catholicism and Pentecostalism – in both their theology and practice – offer correctives to this tendency.

In inner-city contexts such as Shadwell in east London (the location of our final case study), there are particular opportunities for churches from these different denominations to work together on housing. When we build together, there is a mutual enrichment – and we become more than the sum of our parts.

Catholic Perspectives on the Housing Crisis

Pope Francis and the Teología del Pueblo

From the first sermon after his election, Pope Francis challenged the Church to ensure its contribution to discussions of social justice was grounded in both prayer and in the lives of the poorest. This double grounding is also evident in the teaching of his predecessor.

In *Caritas in Veritate* Benedict XVI emphasizes the importance of prayer as a foundation for social action – writing that such action 'requires attention to the spiritual life, a serious consideration of the experiences of trust in God, spiritual fellowship in Christ, reliance upon God's providence and mercy, love and forgiveness, self-denial, acceptance of others, justice and peace. All this is essential if "hearts of stone" are to be transformed into "hearts of flesh".'[1]

In a like manner, Benedict XVI emphasizes the importance of grounding social action in the lives of the poorest. His trilogy entitled *Jesus of Nazareth* repeatedly emphasizes the poverty of Jesus and the disciples that he gathers. Commenting on the infancy narratives, he writes that the glory of God is not rendered visible, 'so that one might say unequivocally "this is the true Lord of the world". Far from it . . . God's poverty is his real sign.'[2] Likewise, in his reflections on the Beatitudes, Benedict notes: 'The setting in which Luke frames the Sermon on the Mount clarifies to whom the Beatitudes are addressed: "He lifted his eyes on his disciples." The individual Beatitudes are the fruit of this looking upon the disciples: They *are* poor, hungry, weeping: they *are* hated and persecuted.'[3]

In *Laudato Si'*, Francis applies these two insights to the specific issue of housing. This encyclical takes its title from a prayer of St Francis of Assisi, and the Pope reminds us that our treatment of our neighbours and of the material world will reflect our understanding of its origins and purpose:

> If we approach nature and the environment without . . . openness and wonder, if we no longer speak the language of fraternity and beauty in our relationship with the world, our attitude will be that of masters, consumers, ruthless exploiters, unable to set limits on their immediate needs. By contrast, if we feel intimately united with all that exists, then sobriety and care will well up spontaneously.[4]

Francis goes on to relate this to the way towns and cities are designed and built – what he calls their 'human ecology':

> The planning of our cities needs to respect and nurture both eco-systems: There is . . . a need to protect those common areas, visual landmarks and urban landscapes which increase our sense of belonging, of rootedness, of 'feeling at home' within a city which includes us and brings us together. It is important that the different parts of a city be well integrated and that those who live there have a sense of the whole, rather than being confined to one neighbourhood and failing to see the larger city as space which they share with others.[5]

A city in which the poorest are forced into outer urban ghettoes – out of sight and out of mind – expresses an idolatrous value system. *Laudato Si'* makes a connection between the state of people's hearts and the way the poorest in society are housed. If the design of our cities reflects the belief that all lives are sacred, then the poorest will not be hidden away. Indeed, they will have a voice in the design of the neighbourhoods in which they live, and the wider 'human ecology' of their towns and cities. They will 'no longer be seen as strangers, but as part of a "we" which all of us are working to create'.

In articulating a vision of a Church that is of (and not only *with* or *for*) the poorest, Pope Francis has drawn on the *teología del pueblo* that has developed in the Latin Amercian Church. As Victor Fernandez explains, this theology

> regard[s] the poor not merely as the object of liberation or education, but as individuals capable of thinking in their own categories, capable of living the faith legitimately in their own manner, capable of forging paths based on their popular culture. Indeed, the fact that they express themselves or look at life differently does not mean that they do not think or have no culture; it is simply a different culture, one that differs from that of the middle class.[6]

While Pope Francis has encountered opposition from conservative elements in the Church, his approach has also disconcerted middle-class liberal, left-wing voices. Rafael Luciano writes:

> More than a few voices have been raised questioning the presence of the option for the people in the teaching of Pope Francis; some even regard it as populist. Many of the criticisms have come from highly educated sociocultural contexts, even from persons who, while they are concerned about the situation of the poor today, have never dealt personally with them or shared their lives.[7]

In an interview in *El Pais*, Francis made clear he does not view 'populism' as a necessarily negative term. As he observed, it has very different meanings in different contexts:

> In Latin America, it means that the people – for instance, people's movements – are the protagonists. They are self-organized. When I started to hear about populism in Europe I didn't know what to make of it, until I realized that it had different meanings.[8]

In Francis's words, 1930s Germany represented a disordered form of 'populism' in which people did not 'talk among themselves' but rather sought refuge from their fears in a 'charismatic leader'. This disordered populism exploits and exacerbates popular resentment, without redistributing either wealth or power from elite groups to the wider populace.

The only effective response to this disordered populism is the other kind of populism envisaged by Francis – a populism in which ordinary people are 'self-organized'.[9] The practice of community organizing, described in the case study below, exemplifies this authentic and inclusive populism.

Catholic social action: a case study

Lucy Achola was a mother of three who was facing eviction from her home. She worshipped in St Stephen's Catholic Church in Manor Park, east London. If the eviction had gone ahead her displacement would have huge consequences: it would mean that she would move far from the place where her two daughters sing in the school choir and her son is an altar server. Ultimately, she would be left without a place to live, away from her friends and community.

As Dunstan Rodrigues explains, it was the parish's engagement in community organizing (see boxed text overleaf) that both addressed her immediate crisis, and developed her as a leader.

> Fortuitously, at the same time, her parish church was engaged in a listening campaign around housing. Through a one-to-one conversation, her story became known, and she was asked to share her testimony along with three others with the local councillor at an accountability assembly hosted in the Church. The acknowledgement of her struggle itself gave her hope and joy: as she put it, 'I was so happy – the whole Parish was behind me.'[10]

The experience of support and solidarity from the parish led Lucy and her family to respond with generosity to another person in need:

[As] she put it, 'God really opened the door.' At a prayer meeting soon after, she meditated with others on the words in the Gospel – 'Be merciful as your heavenly Father is merciful' and St Peter's exhortation: 'Be hospitable' (Luke 6.36, 1 Pet. 4.9). She gave thanks for what she had experienced, and felt moved to welcome one lady facing homelessness into her home, and then welcomed another – offering them both comfort and support.[11]

In addition to offering hospitality to one person, Lucy played a leading role in a community organizing assembly that held the Olympic Legacy Agency to account on the amount of affordable housing on the site of the 2012 Games in east London.

Lucy's story illustrates the way in which community organizing begins with people's immediate concerns (an urgent crisis in housing for a family) and, through an experience of solidarity, enables inner-city residents to become powerful and confident in showing hospitality and campaigning for justice. It also illustrates the way in which organizing enables inner-city worshippers to root their action for justice in their wider spiritual life.

Community organizing brings churches of different denominations – including Anglicans, Roman Catholics and Pentecostals – together with other local religious and civic institutions to act for social justice.

1 Beginning with relationships – Community organizing begins with relationships. Face-to-face meeting and intentional listening come before action.
2 Realism – Community organizing is inspired by a vision of the 'world as it should be', but believes that meaning well is not enough. We need to understand the 'world as it is', so our action has a genuine impact. That is also why, in building relationships, we identify the actual interests and passions of our neighbours – and work on the issues where these interests and passions are shared.

---

3 Being positive about power – Community organizing seeks to build relational power: the ability of citizens to act with others to change their neighbourhoods for the better. Power can be abused, but Christians involved in organizing understand it to be a God-given capacity which we should develop and use together.

4 Committed to developing leaders – Community organizing understands a true 'leader' to be someone who listens to, works with, and develops the potential of others. It builds power by identifying leaders through face-to-face meetings, and developing them through training and action.

5 Beginning with what unites us – Community organizing seeks to build relational power in the most deprived and diverse communities, by encouraging neighbours to focus on their common concerns and aspirations. This means that when people of different faiths and cultures face issues of disagreement, we do so as friends and not strangers.

6 Willing to generate tension – Community organizing recognizes that change usually involves a struggle. We must be willing to generate tension in order to achieve social justice, but that tension is always deployed to achieve a deeper and more lasting harmony; the true peace (shalom) that can only come when there is justice.

7 Teaching through experience and action – Community organizing seeks to develop leaders and congregations through experience. It cultivates a habit of creative, intentional action – so that new relationships are constantly being built, and local leaders are constantly developing their capacities. While a high value is placed on reflection and research, these are always engaged in to improve the quality and focus of action, and not to be a substitute for it.

Pentecostal Perspectives on the Housing Crisis

Pentecostalism: origins and features

Pentecostalism emerged not as the activity of a single human being or group, but as a movement of the Holy Spirit – characterized by charismatic phemomena such as divine healing and speaking in tongues – very often among those most marginalized and oppressed by the wider society, and indeed by many of their fellow Christians.

In the early part of the twentieth century, prayer meetings led by the preacher William Seymour, the son of slaves in a racially violent and deeply segregated society, was the catalyst for the Azusa Street Revival in Los Angeles. These gatherings in the initial period were characterized by multiculturalism and the leadership of women – two features that were revolutionary in the social and political context of the times.

As Ruthlyn Bradshaw explains,

> From the beginning, William Seymour, filled with the Holy Spirit and driven with the desire for equality and justice, made a difference by changing the existing order of things. Affecting change was an integral part of the Pentecostal experience from the start.[12]

The Azusa Street Revival, as well as similar revivals in Korea and India, were moments of change for Pentecostal believers. In each of these cases, existing power structures were challenged by what were understood as moves of the Spirit. In Azusa Street, this meant blacks and whites worshipping together; in India, this meant Dalits being welcomed as brothers and sisters; in Korea, it meant indigenous leaders being recognized as equals to European missionaries. The work of the Spirit is seen as powerful, not only within the life of the individual, but as a force for challenging inequalities and injustices within and beyond the Church.

Since the 1950s, Afro-Caribbean migrants have changed the face of the English Church by bringing their Pentecostal faith with them.[13] Hugh Osgood describes four 'demographic strands' of Pentecostal congregations in the UK. He recognizes two kinds of 'indigenous' (white) church; those birthed in the early 1900s and charismatic churches started during the 1960s onwards. He then highlights three kinds of church made up of ethnic minorities, including those linked to Caribbean migration of the 1950s and 1960s (the postwar immigration from the colonies, now known as the Windrush era); those established as a result of African migration in the 1960s and again in the 1980s and 1990s; and those formed by new migrants to the UK.[14]

Afro-Caribbean migrants in Britain have faced the hostility, injustice and even violence that many groups of people have faced in different times and places around the world. These women and men, many of whom considered themselves to be 'reverse missionaries', often found themselves among the poorest and most disadvantaged in the British population.[15] There are many stories of the earliest arrivals from the Caribbean being met with the racism of their white Christian brothers and sisters in the faith who refused to welcome them. As Pentecostal scholar Walter Hollenweger expresses it, 'Christians in Britain prayed for many years for revival, and when it came they did not recognize it because it was black.'[16]

In her commentary on the Acts of the Apostles, Beverley Roberts Gaventa observes that the 'acts' that are recorded in the book are more accurately described as the acts of *God* through the apostles.[17] The Holy Spirit is the primary agent: the apostles' ministry begins when the Spirit descends upon them, and at key moments in the Church's discernment (for example, on whether Gentiles can be baptized, or whether all foods are clean) it is the direct action of the Spirit that charts the way for the disciples.

The lively expectation of the Spirit's presence and action in the world is central to Pentecostal action for social justice. The community of the Church is formed by the Spirit's action. As Pentecostal theologian Stanko Jambrek explains, believers with a Pentecostal experience consider it very important to have fellowship based on the Word of God and permeated with the action of doing God's will. Fellowship is created by God and Christians: God reveals His will, and the Christians fulfil it.[18]

Pentecostal social action therefore shares a number of characteristics with Catholic Social Teaching and practice: it is rooted in the lives of the poorest, and it both expects and bears witness to the activity of the Holy Spirit in their midst. In the life of many Pentecostal churches in England's poorest neighbourhoods, we see the reality that Victor Fernandez described in Latin America – of 'the poor not merely as the object of liberation or education' but as active agents, 'capable of thinking in their own categories, capable of living the faith legitimately in their own manner, capable of forging paths based on their popular culture'.

In Pentecostal congregations, the will of God is revealed as the community offers accountability, correction and confirmation – discerning, celebrating and sharing the work God is doing in their midst. The practices of fasting, communal story telling, vibrant corporate worship and prophecy are all central to Pentecostal life. In the next section, we explore the ways in which they are integrated with social action in a holistic vision of the Church's life and mission.

Pentecostal spirituality and social action

The spiritual discipline of *fasting* is a means of purifying the believer's interior spiritual life, to draw closer to God, and is often exercised in times of trial or to make key life decisions. Pentecostals often exercise this spiritual discipline in both private and corporate ways and are often an annual event in the calendar of the Church and the life of the believer, even from childhood. Fasting is also used to navigate through extreme difficulty, to fight spiritual and social darkness, and Jesus' advice in Mark 9.29 that 'this kind only comes out through prayer and fasting' is regularly used to affirm this activity.

To give a specific example, a Pentecostal church in Birmingham encountered a rogue landlord who operated a self-converted brothel next door to the church gates. This abusive form of housing and exploitation towards vulnerable women alarmed many of the church members and a week's course of fasting commenced. A striking feature of this church's emergency fast was the tangible expectation and anticipation that God would show up to defend the vulnerable women, would provide solutions, and there would be a story of victory at the end of the fast. The result was a remarkable chain of events that led to the closure of the brothel and the bringing of the rogue landlord to justice. The victories of this fast were spread through public testimony and were integrated into Sunday sermons. To this day, church members will remind one another of this answered prayer to encourage and provide assurance of God's immanence.

Such *communal story telling* in Pentecostal churches is a common practice of encouragement for believers. Whole planned services, usually in the evening, are dedicated to hearing the testimonies of a believer's week or month and serve as a platform for the laity to publicly express God's faithfulness. Testimonies also affirm God's present activity, relevance and reduce the temptation to objectify God as an ancient mythical character or transcendent being with no direct engagement in the life experiences of his creation. They also allow people who the wider society oppresses and marginalizes to tell their own story, and celebrate their place as beloved and chosen children of God.

The *vibrant corporate worship* of Pentecostals also helps them recognize and celebrate God's active presence in the world. The act of praise and worship that was exercised by the Jewish worshippers in front of the walls of Jericho influences the way that Pentecostals link prayer, praise and worship with justice and action – challenging the 'walls' of contemporary oppression and injustice.

Prophecy is a spiritual office that has recently regained prominence in Pentecostal churches. In its correct use for reproof, guidance and being a mouthpiece for God's word, it is a tangible expression of God's guidance in the world – calling out injustice and revealing God's active presence and concern about the wider social and political climate, instead of being hijacked by the avaricious and unbiblical agenda of the prosperity gospel. Faithful prophecy helps Pentecostals to sense where God is and what God wants them to do as agents of change in this present world. Prophecies are discerned and weighed – both for their faithfulness to Scripture and for signs of independent confirmation.

The case study below is drawn from the Church of God of Prophecy (COGOP), whose action on housing emerged out of a process of discernment that involved all of these spiritual disciplines.

Pentecostal action: a case study

Nehemiah United Churches Housing Association (NUCHA) was started in Birmingham by Pentecostal church leaders who were increasingly aware of the needs of their congregation members and the lack of local provision. The biblical story of Nehemiah resonates with the mission of NUCHA which is not only to provide housing but to 'build communities'.[19] NUCHA started in the 1980s and is now the largest provider of housing by black Pentecostals in the UK.

Bishop Wilton Powell explains that he began to question whether the pastoral focus of his ministry fell short of responding in a long-term and practical way to the needs of a member of his congregation who was elderly, had many health concerns, and was isolated in inadequate housing.[20] Leaders across the network of COGOP, as well as Pastor Corbett and a group of leaders from other Pentecostal denominations, recognized that housing provision was culturally inadequate for elderly people from black, Asian and ethnic minority backgrounds. Both groups responded entrepreneurially, gathering professionals and experts from among their congregations, to start housing associations. Nehemiah Housing Association and the United Churches Housing Association both launched in the 1980s through the initiative of leaders within COGOP and those outside the denomination, respectively. Having accomplished great work over almost 30 years, they merged in 2007 to form NUCHA.

Bishop Llewelyn Graham, the CEO of the housing association, was one of the talented individuals who was recruited to be involved at the outset. He explains his sense of vocation to this ministry which has caused him to be known as bishop not of the Church, but of the community: 'It wasn't about those natural and temporal things like money and security, it was about an opportunity to fulfil that sense of the call of God, and something that would honour my grandmother, by being able to take care of the elderly'.[21]

Leaders within COGOP in Birmingham, who named the Housing Association after the biblical figure Nehemiah, recognized him as one who was 'for those people who are distressed, in poverty, imprisoned and isolated and who felt that they had to . . . re-establish their communities'.[22]

However, along with this desire to care is a deep sense of justice and an implicit belief in human dignity and human agency. As Caribbean migrants, the leaders of NUCHA suffered the hostility that was common for many who arrived in the 1950s and 1960s in Britain. Bishop Llewellyn explains that it was the experiences of church members on the ground, as well as the political atmosphere at the time, which acted as catalyst for the birth of both housing associations:

> The Commission of Racial Equality (CRE) did some research about racism in Britain and it was published around about the same time about the lack of adequate housing for our community . . . the government responded by instructing the then Housing Corporation to look at developing a strategy in response to that report about racism in housing.[23]

The response by churches was to organize in order to tackle this issue themselves. Alongside caring for the elderly and those from all backgrounds with housing needs, NUCHA offered an opportunity for community development. Bishop Wilton

Powell explains that 'we also had a vision for our development as a community, empowering our people and our church, moving from the margins and advocating in a wider sense'.

Pentecostal action today

In the 31 years since NUCHA was founded, Pentecostalism has become a more confident and established presence in the English Church.

In the USA, African American Pentecostal and Baptist churches – shaped by the civil rights struggle – stand at the heart of community-organizing campaigns on issues such as the Living Wage, controlling the availability of guns, and affordable housing.

Pentecostal and Baptist churches are at the heart of East Brooklyn Congregations – a community-organizing alliance in New York – and have pioneered the Nehemiah Housing strategy to replace hundreds of acres of blighted, abandoned housing with large-scale developments of new, high-quality housing that is affordable for ownership by low- and moderate-income residents of those communities. Over 4,500 Nehemiah Homes have been built in East New York, and over 1,000 in the South Bronx.

Robert Beckford argues that Pentecostal churches in England have as yet failed to achieve this level of social impact because they have often internalized the very oppressive attitudes and hierarchies that contributed to their oppression.[24] In more recent times, the 'prosperity gospel' – often rooted in American capitalism and exported to other parts of the world – undermines liberation movements globally. By exalting the individual pursuit of wealth, without questioning its social and ecological cost, and seeking to justify it by distorting the content of the faith, it mirrors many of the pathologies of colonialism. Beckford has urged Caribbean Pentecostals to take on the 'active radicalism' first described in the work of Valentina Alexander 'to more effectively undermine the oppressive hegemonic practices of society, which in its latent state it could only attempt to cope with or survive under'.[25]

Alexander and Beckford are challenging Pentecostals to resist the privatization of the gospel, and its detachment from social justice – and also to reach back into the foundational experiences of the movement, in which the Holy Spirit's action converted individuals, formed a church whose common life ran counter to the racial and social segregation of the day, and challenged structural injustice in the wider society. It is when Christians are expectant and receptive to all three dimensions of the Spirit's work that the most profound transformation is possible.

Building Together: A Case Study

Both in their theology and practice, Catholicism and Pentecostalism invite the wider Church to ensure that we build housing *together* – together with God, and together with those in greatest need of justice, who are always at the heart of the Spirit's work. We want to conclude with a case study that shows what can happen when an Anglican parish accepts that invitation; when some of the insights of Catholic and Pentecostal social action are combined with a distinctively Anglican commitment to place.

In April 2016, the congregation of St George-in-the-East had their first experience of a community-organizing assembly. Members of this Anglican church in Shadwell joined 6,000 other Londoners to secure commitments from the Mayoral candidates on affordable housing. These included a redefinition of 'affordability' (tying it to a percentage of the average local wage, rather than of the average market price for a home) and a commitment to build 1,000 homes in Community Land Trusts (a form of locally led affordable housing that ensures it remains so in perpetuity). The agenda presented to the Mayoral candidates had emerged out of tens of thousands of 'one-to-one' conversations in Citizens UK's member institutions across the capital. These had identified housing as the top issue of concern, and shaped the specific agenda for action.

Organizing enabled a local church to have the power of

a city-wide alliance, while remaining firmly anchored in the context of its neighbourhood. 'One-to-ones' within the congregation, and among neighbours in Darul Ummah Mosque and the parish school (St Paul's Whitechapel), had identified housing as the main local concern. In June 2016, worshippers from St George's and the nearby Darul Ummah went on a Walk for Affordable Housing – and identified a large, unsightly piece of land just minutes from the church. After some research, it emerged that this land was the 'jewel in the crown' of Transport for London's (TfL) Small Sites Programme, and was likely to be sold off for luxury housing. Over the next 18 months, local people worked together to build support for a Community Land Trust (CLT) on the site – a form of housing that ensures the price of homes is linked in perpetuity to average local incomes.

Alongside the process of community listening, St George's weekly cycle of worship has been reshaped to have a focus on *receptivity* – on discerning where the Spirit is already at work in the lives of both the gathered congregation and the wider parish.

The campaign was deeply integrated with the congregation's worship: in Holy Week, St George's Palm Sunday procession stopped at the site to pray for the campaign. In June, a packed assembly in the church persuaded Tower Hamlets Mayor John Biggs to back the plan for a CLT – after some powerful testimony on the impact of inadequate housing on family life, and a rather tense public negotiation between Mayor Biggs and Fr Richard Springer (one of St George's priests). In December, children from the school recorded a Christmas video with testimony explaining why affordable housing mattered to them and their families.

In March 2018, it was confirmed that the site will be developed not as luxury flats, but entirely as a CLT. As a result of the campaign, 100 local people will be housed in affordable, good-quality housing. Crucially, this campaign has not just had a heart *for* those suffering in London's housing crisis. Those who need homes have been at its heart. It has built their confidence – both in their individual capabilities, and in the potential of collective action. It has also drawn more people into the church's worshipping life, perhaps because of the connections drawn in homilies, Bible study and liturgy between faith and social action.

Through some of the relationships developed between church and mosque, 'The Open Table' project developed – in which Muslims and Christians, homeless and housed, share a common meal. The project began with participants preparing and sharing a monthly meal in the church building, but it became clear that many homeless people in the neighbourhood were intimidated by the imposing building, and reluctant to enter it. The group therefore decided to take the table out on to the streets each week – going to where homeless people were, instead of always expecting them to come into St George's. A further striking feature of The Open Table is that many of those who are now serving food to homeless people in Shadwell have themselves experienced homelessness or other forms of marginalization and oppression.

The commitment of The Open Table to genuine mutuality is leading participants on to two further questions: how can community organizing in Shadwell include homeless people, so that they can be active leaders in the fight for the accommodation and support that they need? And what does it mean for the church to recognize that homeless people may well have a faith, and need spiritual care?

When one of the church members who is a key leader in The Open Table told a homeless person that the church was not trying to convert them, he replied: 'Why not? Am I not welcome in church?' The wider leadership of St George's has begun to reflect on what would have to change to make its Sunday worship more fully inclusive of homeless worshippers.

Research by Lemos and Crane has shown that, in their anxiety not to link social care with proselytism, the (often religious) agencies that provide for homeless people often fail to address their spiritual needs.[26] For St George's and other congregations like it to treat homeless people as equals will involve recognizing that some of them are already members of the Body of Christ, and others may be interested in joining it.

As we have seen, Pentecostals expect God to be present and active in the material world. There is a strong Pentecostal presence in the leadership of The Open Table with some coming from black-majority Pentecostal churches and others having experienced Roman Catholic worship influenced by Pentecostalism. This fusion of spiritualities has led to an expectation of, and attentiveness to, the activity of the Spirit (which is then shared and celebrated through testimony and story telling) and a focus on corporate action for justice where (in Pope Francis's words) 'the people are the protagonists'.

The work of The Open Table, and St George's wider campaigning on housing, is transforming church members' understanding of social action. The combination of a rhythm of prayer that emphasizes discernment with a form of social engagement that emphasizes the agency of the poorest is helping this Anglican parish to receive some of the gifts Roman Catholicism and Pentecostalism can offer the wider Body.

Notes

1 *Caritas in Veritate*, 79.

2 Benedict XVI (2012), *Jesus of Nazareth: The Infancy Narratives*, London: Bloomsbury, p. 79.

3 Benedict XVI (2008), *Jesus of Nazareth: From the Baptism in the Jordan to the Transfiguration*, London: Bloomsbury, p. 70.

4 *Laudato Si'*, 11.

5 *Laudato Si'*, 151.

6 Rodari, P. (2014), 'Conversaciones con Víctor Manuel Fernández', *Iglesia Viva* 259, July–September, p. 65, quoted in Luciani, R. (2017), *Pope Francis and the Theology of the People*, New York: Orbis Books, p. 9.

7 Luciani, *Pope*, p. 9.

8 Pope Francis (2017), interview in *El Pais*, 21 January, online at https://elpais.com/elpais/2017/01/21/inenglish/1485026427_223988.html.

9 Bretherton, L. (2015), *Resurrecting Democracy: Faith, Citizenship and the Politics of a Common Life*, chapter 1, New York: Cambridge University Press; Ritchie, A. (2019), *Inclusive Populism: Creating Citizens in the Global Age*, South Bend, IN: University of Notre Dame Press.

10 Rodrigues, D. (2018), *Realities are Greater than Ideas: Evangelisation, Catholicism and Community Organising*, London: Centre for Theology and Community, p. 25.

11 Rodrigues, *Realities*.

12 The Revd Ruthlyn Bradshaw, 'Pentecostal Hermeneutics', at the Dr Oliver Lyseight Annual Lecture at NTCG, February 2010, www.ntcg.org.uk/education/2010annuallecture-bradshaw.stm (accessed 8.8.14).

13 Woodhead, L. and Catto, R., eds (2012), *Religion and Change in Modern Britain*, Oxford/New York: Routledge, p. 71.

14 Osgood, H., *Internal Briefing for Churches Together in England*, www.cte.org.uk/Groups/248695/Home/Resources/Pentecostal_and_Multicultural/The_Pentecostal_and/The_Pentecostal_and.aspx (accessed 30.1.20).

15 This concept has been picked up in Olofinjana, I. (2019), *Reverse Mission: Towards an African British Theology: Transformation*, https://doi.org/10.1177/0265378819877902. It is also seen in Calley, M. (1965), *God's People: West Indian Pentecostal Sects in England*, Oxford: Oxford University Press, p. 30 (accessed 26.2.20).

16 Hollenweger, W. (1992), Foreword by R. I. H. Gerloff, *A Plea for British Black Theologies: The Black Church Movement in Britain in its Transatlantic, Cultural and Theological Interaction*, Frankfurt: Peter Lang, p. ix.

17 Roberts Gaventa, B. (2003), *Abingdon New Testament Commentaries: Acts of the Apostles* (Nashville, TN: Abingdon Press).

18 Jambrek, S. (2008), *Unity and Fellowship Of Christians From A Pentecostal Perspective*, ebook (reprint, Bible Institute, Zagreb), p. 68, http://file:///C:/Users/Sarah/Downloads/06_Jambrek.pdf (accessed 4.3.20).

19 'About Us' on the NHA website http://nehemiah-ucha.co.uk/page.php?id=2 (accessed 8.11.19).

20 Interview with Bishop Wilton Powell, Birmingham, July 2019.

21 Interview with Bishop Llewelyn Graham, CEO of NHA, Birmingham, July 2019.

22 Interview with Bishop Wilton Powell, Birmingham, July 2019.

23 Interview with Bishop Llewellyn Graham, Birmingham, July 2019.

24 Beckford, R. (2000), *Dread and Pentecostal: A Political Theology for the Black Church in Britain*, Eugene, OR: Wipf and Stock.

25 Alexander, V. (1997), 'Breaking Every Fetter? To what extent has the Black-led church in Britain developed a Theology of Liberation?', PhD thesis, University of Warwick, pp. 273–4.

26 Gravell, C. (2013), *Lost and Found: Faith and Spirituality in the Lives of Homeless People*, London: Lemos & Crane.

7

The Integrity of Creatureliness: Materiality, Flourishing, and Housing

NIAMH COLBROOK

We are material creatures. As material creatures, we make our dwellings within and as part of the material world, cooperating with the qualities and processes of that world as we build our shelters, homes and neighbourhoods. Our materiality is, as we shall see, central to our ability to flourish: to grow, change, and learn in relationship with other creatures. Yet we also suffer in our materiality where our basic needs go unmet, where our lives become dominated by pain or illness, or where we become bound to habits or systems that diminish us.

The housing crisis raises the relationship between materiality, flourishing and suffering to a level of urgency. Not only do we lack sufficient housing to meet the needs of a growing population but, in 2018, 4.3 million households – around a sixth – were living in 'non-decent' homes. One million homes were deemed 'unfit for human habitation', posing serious risks to health.[1]

The housing crisis highlights the cyclical nature of inequality. Empirical studies have long established the relationship between housing and wellbeing, in particular the negative impact of poor housing on physical and mental health. Insufficient access to affordable, good-quality housing is a primary factor in generating health inequality.[2] Indoor air pollution and damp, often caused by poor heating and ventilation, significantly increase the likelihood of developing severe respiratory illness, particularly among children.[3] Warmer houses, meanwhile, are correlated to higher school and work attendance.[4]

The material conditions of housing have similar effects on mental and emotional wellbeing. Poor-quality housing is correlated to long-term mental health problems.[5] High house prices and rental costs increase financial instability and can lead to cycles of debt that further damage mental wellbeing.[6] Often unable to extricate themselves from damaging environments, individuals can become bound to cycles that mark the course of their lives.[7] Worsening physical and mental health, for example, may lead to precarious employment prospects, rendering individuals dependent on government benefit schemes and social housing systems that may deteriorate their wellbeing further.[8]

The relationship between housing and flourishing is not reducible to the quality of individual properties alone. Qualitative studies draw attention to a nested set of material problems spanning the home and the broader neighbourhood. Poor living conditions are often worsened by difficult relationships with landlords or local councils. Tenants report, for example, unreliable responses to complaints and maintenance requests, concerning not only individual homes, but also the cleanliness and safety of apartment blocks.[9] Individuals report problems such as conflict among neighbours, including threats of violence, drug abuse and crime, leading to fear for the safety of adults and children alike.[10] Residents also highlight the lack of safe outdoor space for play and exercise, the provision of which is connected to not only healthy childhood development, but also adult mental wellbeing.[11]

The housing crisis, then, brings us face-to-face with the systemic inequalities that impede flourishing both in the short- and long-term, and their emergence in and through our relationships with our material environments. These connections between housing and flourishing are, we have seen, well established in the empirical literature. This literature gives us insight into how these systems of injustice take shape, but it does not ask why our material nature binds us to patterns of suffering. If we are to respond to the housing crisis, we must be able to say not only *that* materiality and suffering are related, but *how* they are related. What is it about the kinds of creatures we are that renders our flourishing so inseparable from our material environments?

In this chapter, I respond to this question by offering a theological approach to the connection between materiality, flourishing and suffering, rooted in a concept of creatureliness. I begin with the doctrine of creation, before unpacking its implications for an account of the integrity of creatureliness, a concept I will define below. Through this account of integrity, I argue that all creatures flourish in their particular natures through material interdependence with creation as a whole. I then turn to discuss human flourishing and human sin, arguing that the relationship between materiality and suffering can be more easily grasped on the basis of this theological account of creaturely flourishing. Finally, I suggest how this theological vision offers a framework within which Christians may discern concrete responses to the housing crisis, through reframing the character of the problems we face and, in the process, providing hope for healing.

Creator and Creation

The concept of creatureliness makes no sense apart from a doctrine of creation. To be a creature is to be in relationship with the creator. We must establish the nature of that relationship before discussing creatureliness further. How we describe that relationship depends, in turn, on who or what we take to be the creator, and what it means to create and be created.

Christian reflection on the character of God follows in the footsteps of the Hebrew Scriptures, which repeatedly characterize God as the creator. For one thing, this means that God is 'in the beginning', forming the world. But the doctrine of creation is not only a story of cosmic origins. The Hebrew Scriptures seem less concerned with pinpointing the technicalities of these origins than with the character of the God who is called creator, the God who can be trusted to redeem.

Throughout the books of Isaiah and Psalms, for example, the creative and salvific power of God are spoken together. As Psalm 124.8 proclaims, 'Our help is in the name of the LORD, who made heaven and earth.'[12]

This concern takes on a particular hue as early Christians begin to read the Hebrew Scriptures as the book of Christ. In this light, the creative and salvific power of God is revealed first and foremost in the incarnation. John's Gospel, for example, re-tells the creation narrative in a Christological idiom. The Word who was 'in the beginning', through whom all things came into being, is the Word who takes on flesh and dwells among us (John 1.1–14). Elsewhere, Christ is called the 'first-born of all creation', for 'all things have been created through him and for him. He himself is before all things, and in him all things hold together' (Col. 1.15–17). Christ, through whom all things were created, takes on flesh in order to offer healing and re-creation. Through this work, the Holy Spirit draws creation to be re-formed in new life; the Spirit rests on the disciples at Pentecost (Acts 2.3) just as the Spirit hovered over the formless creation in the beginning (Gen. 1.2).

Creation and salvation are both the outworking of the one will of God, the God revealed as Trinity. To speak of God as 'creator' is to say, in the words of the Nicene-Constantin-opolitan creed, that we believe in One God: the Father, the Almighty, maker of heaven and earth; one Lord, Jesus Christ through whom all things were made; and the Holy Spirit, the Lord, the giver of life.

The Scriptures themselves do not provide technical descriptions of how God creates. This question becomes increasingly important, though, if we are to witness to the character of the God who is revealed as creator. It is possible, as the history of the Church attests, to affirm God as creator in a number of ways, each of which tells a different story not only about the character of the material world, but also about the character of God.

The question of the meaning of creation became particularly heated in the second century, when Christians were faced with controversies surrounding the nature and character of the material world. Perhaps the most significant question in this period concerned the status of matter in relation to God. Broadly speaking, Platonist philosophies described the origin of the world as the 'ordering of unformed matter'.[13] This matter was different to God, but not created by God. Creation was framed as the process whereby God brought the world into being from this unformed matter. God's creative power provided it with order and form, a kind of salvation from its own inherent chaos and instability. The imperfections associated with the material world were simply a result of the deficiency of matter itself.[14]

The doctrine of creation from nothing emerged in this context. This doctrine affirms that God created all that exists from nothing. God does not depend on anything outside Godself in order to create, and thus everything that exists, including matter, has its beginning and its being in God. The rejection of an eternal, uncreated matter stemmed from the need to safeguard the particularity of the God revealed through Jesus Christ and the Scriptures. As Ian McFarland puts it, 'the doctrine of creation from nothing . . . emerges as the only account of the world's origin that does justice to the Christian conviction that there is only one God'.[15] If God is dependent on something outside Godself in order to create, we cannot maintain the all-sufficiency of God's will and power. If God is constrained by some external force, God depends on something or someone else in order to be God the creator.

By the same logic, the doctrine of creation from nothing also allows us to maintain the intimate scriptural connection between creation and salvation. Limiting God's power to create raises questions about God's power to save. If God's power is insufficient for the creation of matter, can it be sufficient for the gift of new life? The doctrine of creation from nothing affirms, in this way, the centrality of grace to the Christian faith. To say that God creates from nothing is to say that nothing in us, nothing in the world, and nothing in existence could compel God to create. Creation is a gift. So too is salvation a gift. Just as nothing can compel God to create, nothing can compel God to save. Moreover, because God's loving power depends on nothing outside of God's own nature, nothing can separate us from the love of God (Rom. 8.39).[16]

The God with whose worship the Scriptures resound is the God of grace, the God who creates out of love. The doctrine of creation from nothing speaks of this all-sufficient love as the very ground of existence. If this is the character of the creator, and what it means for God to create, the concept of creatureliness takes on a distinctive shape. Julian of Norwich beautifully expresses such a vision of creatureliness:

> [God showed me] a little thing, the size of a hazelnut, on the palm of my hand, round like a ball. I looked at it thoughtfully and wondered, 'What is this?' And the answer came, 'It is all that is made.' I marvelled that it continued to exist and did not suddenly disintegrate; it was so small. And again my mind supplied the answer, 'It exists, both now and forever, because God loves it.' In short, everything owes its existence to the love of God. In this 'little thing' I saw three truths. The first is that God made it; the second is that God loves it; and the third is that God sustains it.[17]

The intimate presence of God is the very condition of all being, not only at its beginning, but at every moment of its existence. As Janet Soskice summarizes, 'the world is graced in its createdness, which is happening all the time'.[18]

The Integrity of Creatureliness: Materiality and Flourishing

The doctrine of creation from nothing sketches the contours of a concept of creatureliness through insisting that creation is a work of grace, always dependent on the love of God. We can now develop a fuller vision of the nature of material creatures, and how they flourish in relation to their material nature. I develop this connection between creatureliness, materiality and flourishing through the concept of integrity. Integrity refers both to what something is, its nature or character; and

114

to how something is, the way it exists as itself. In the unity of these two senses of integrity we can perceive the relationship between materiality and flourishing.

If we are to understand the integrity of creatureliness, we must be guided by a basic tenet of the doctrine of creation: creatures are not God. This claim may seem absurdly obvious, but it tells us a good deal about the distinctive nature of creatures. God is infinite, enduring 'from everlasting to everlasting' (Ps. 90.2), unlimited by time or place. There is nothing more that God could become, and thus God is always fully Godself. Creatures are finite. They grow into their natures; their material existence takes time. While God is perfect in divinity, creatures are called to a goodness particular to their material finitude. First and foremost, then, the doctrine of creation teaches us that it is good for creatures to be finite: limited by time and space, measurable and countable, and changeable.

What creatures are, as material and finite, is inseparable from how they characteristically exist. Augustine of Hippo offers us an account of creatureliness that draws out this dual sense of integrity:

> Things rise and set: in their emerging they begin as it were to be, and grow to perfection; having reached perfection, they grow old and die . . . That is the law limiting their being. So much [has God] given them, namely to be parts of things which do not all have their being at the same moment, but by passing away and successiveness, they all form the whole of which they are parts.[19]

Material creatures come to be at a particular time and have a natural end. Between these points, their existence takes shape through their ability to grow and change, occupying particular places as part of creation as a whole.

It is therefore integral to material creatures that they are part of a community of creation.[20] This community of creation emerges through the distinctive way creatures are called to exist. Limited by time, place and movement, material creatures exist always in relation to other such limited beings. As Augustine puts it, 'it is through things giving way to and taking the place of one another that the beautiful tapestry of the ages is woven'.[21] The mutuality of creaturely becoming means that the integrity of creatureliness is always relationally constituted. As Rowan Williams argues:

> The contents of the world are mutable and passible, and thus are bound to be acted upon by each other, and if the world as a whole is good, then its good must be realised through interactive processes; all things are good in virtue of where they stand in a system of acting upon and being acted upon.[22]

A clarification is required here. It would be easy to misread statements of the relational constitution of creaturely integrity to be suggesting that the value of material creatures is instrumental. That is, that creatures have value only because they achieve some greater purpose within the whole creation. If we are to understand the relationship between materiality and flourishing, we need to demonstrate why reducing creaturely value to instrumental value is inconsistent with the account of creatureliness offered here.

Framing the goodness or value of creatures in instrumental terms would be to mischaracterize the relationship between creator and creation, particularly the relationship between creaturely and divine action. God does not need to create and does not depend on creation to achieve created ends, thus 'if God brings a creature into existence, then that creature must have value in God's sight beyond its instrumentality in giving rise to such effects'.[23] God truly gives creation the ability to act within its own finite capacities, but this power of action is a gift of grace, not a requirement through which creatures earn their keep.

Augustine clarifies his vision of wholes and parts with such a non-instrumental account of value: 'the perfection of every single thing is established, according to the limited measure appropriate to it, not so much in the whole of which it is a part as in him from whom it derived . . . its very being'.[24] The goodness of each creature does not trickle down to it, so to speak, on account of its being part of a larger whole. Creation from nothing teaches that God is immediately present to each creature as the condition of its existence and goodness.

The dual sense of integrity with which we have been concerned can help us to elucidate this nuance, because it allows us to see value in terms of both what a creature is and how it exists. A creature has value simply by virtue of *what* it is, as created, which is to say that it holds ultimate value in God, on whom it depends. A creature also has value in *how* it exists, as finite and material, and thus how it interacts with other creatures as part of a whole, contributing to a common good. Since everything is upheld by the immediate presence of God, all that exists stands in a relationship with the creator that is the condition for its ability to relate to anything else. Precisely because every creature has inherent value, it is given a valuable kind of activity within creation as a whole. This activity is not the source of value in an instrumental sense, but the time-bound refraction of ultimate value in God.

This dual sense of integrity and value culminates in a particular view of the relationship between materiality and flourishing. Augustine's concept of creaturely rest will be instructive here:

> Only [in God] may [the creature] finally come to rest, may it attain, that is, the goal of its own momentum . . . While God abides in himself, he swings everything . . . that comes from him back to himself . . . so that every creature may find in him the goal and terminus of its nature, not to be what he is, but to find in him the place of rest in which to preserve what by nature it is itself.[25]

Creaturely flourishing is the 'rest' the creature finds in God the creator.[26] Augustine's notion of a creaturely 'goal and terminus' does not risk reducing creaturely value to the achievement of an instrumental end, for in their rest creatures 'preserve' what they are 'by nature'.

Yet neither does Augustine separate creaturely value from the creation as a whole. Creaturely rest is also the consummation of how creatures exist: in God, the creature attains 'the goal of its own momentum'. The creator 'swings everything that comes from him back to himself' through the same loving presence that gives creatures the time and space to become themselves. Creatures are therefore called to their rest through the particular forms of activity that are most proper to their nature and, as Augustine has already insisted, this includes their relationships with other creatures.

A creature does not flourish *because* it fulfils some greater purpose in relation to other creatures. A creature flourishes in those relationships because of the character of its graced integrity. It grows in relation to these other creatures because it is inherently good, and because it is the character of its particular, finite goodness that it is realized in relation to others.

Creation is vibrant, alive with desire for God. Material creatures perform this desire through their own diverse kinds of 'momentum', to use Augustine's term, which weave together the 'beauty of the ages'. Flourishing most simply means creatures resting in the love of the creator, the constant condition of their existence, through becoming most fully themselves in God and in creation as a whole.

If flourishing involves a creature being most fully itself, and if finite creatures live out their integrity in relation to others, then flourishing is communal. Creation flourishes as a whole. Finite creatures are bound together by their materiality, thus as one creature flourishes by being and becoming most fully itself, it contributes to the conditions by which another may flourish. We have arrived, therefore, at a dynamic view of the integrity of creatureliness, wherein creation is most itself as a community of activity and agency that finds its source and end in God.

Human Flourishing and Human Sin

Nothing in this theological account of flourishing has thus far demanded a distinction between human and non-human. Through following the logic of a doctrine of creation, I have articulated a relationship between materiality and flourishing that finds its contours in the creator–creature relationship. Flourishing is best understood in relation to creatureliness, and only on this basis in relation to humanness.[27] This vision of creaturely integrity allows us to see that human flourishing emerges through communities of material creatures. It also offers a nuanced account of how systemic forms of suffering become bound up with our material natures.

Humans are material creatures. As such, we are good in accordance with our finitude. We emerge in our particularity in relation to, and dependence on, the communities of creation in which we are always set. These communities afford us our possibilities and capacities for flourishing. Most obviously, we depend upon other material creatures in order to meet our basic needs, such as food, drink and warmth. Through this provision offered by other creatures, we also develop the capacities for diverse forms of flourishing, such as our creativity and our delight in beauty. These capacities do not stand separately from, or over against, the interactive processes of the creation as a whole, but arise because we are embedded in those processes.

Humans are habit-making creatures. Over time, we are materially formed through our practices. As our bodies become habituated to these practices, new capacities emerge.[28] This process takes place in and through our interdependence with other creatures. Take, for example, building practices. Warmth and shelter are basic human needs. In its simplest form, building meets these needs. Skill and artistry in building develop through the gradual cultivation of knowledge born from close, sustained attention to the particular material qualities of the creatures on whom we depend in our building.[29] We learn to build architecture that delights only through these forms of habituation. Human creativity emerges in and through our

119

collaboration with other creatures, and at its best joins with a community of creaturely activity in which each is offered the possibility and capacity to flourish.[30]

This vision is, however, markedly idealized. In reality, humans rarely engage with the world in this way. We have brought destruction and damage through our relationships with other creatures, relationships that have been characterized not by delight in creaturely flourishing, but by abuse of power. Though we may not always see, in practice, the harmonious communities of action I have described, we can only fully appreciate human sin and its effects in the context of this positive vision.

Definitions of sin abound. For the purposes of this discussion, I turn to a description offered by Augustine, chosen for its resonances with the vision of creaturely integrity we have already established:

> The soul, loving its own power, slides away from the whole which is common to all into the part which is its own private property. By following God's directions . . . it could enjoy the whole universe of creation; but by the apostasy of pride which is called the beginning of sin it strives to grab something more than the whole and to govern it by its own laws . . . by being greedy for more it gets less.[31]

Through pride, Augustine suggests, humans have rejected creaturely limitation, setting ourselves over and above our enmeshment in, and dependence on, the creation as a whole. This pride entails a love of power. Humans use their power to exploit the broader creation and 'govern it by [their] own laws', rejecting their nature as part of that whole.

We can never truly extricate ourselves from these material communities. We can, however, live in falsehood. Believing ourselves to be separate from the creation, we treat our fellow creatures as the passive means through which to achieve human ends. Human goods become conceptually separable from the goodness of creation as a whole. The value of other creatures is framed in instrumental terms. Through the short-term gain of greed, we come to believe that our flourishing can stand apart from the flourishing of other creatures.

Sin cannot destroy our creatureliness completely, because it cannot overcome the creative power and love of God. We are irrevocably embedded within communities of creaturely flourishing. This means, however, that our self-destruction is also the destruction of these communities. Sin is most pernicious precisely because it deforms communities of creaturely action. Creation, damaged but not destroyed, continues to unfold as a whole through the interdependence of its parts.

As I have argued above, the wholeness of creation is woven through the finite characteristics of material creatures: their interactions in time and place; and their power to affect, and be affected by, one another. These interactions, I have suggested, allow new capacities for flourishing to emerge and take shape. Sin distorts these good processes like an infection. It spreads through communities of creation, rippling out through broader networks of creaturely interdependence. Creation as a whole continues to take shape through relationships that were intended to allow mutual flourishing. Now, however, these relationships perpetuate harm. Just as flourishing emerges through creaturely communities of agency and activity, so too does suffering emerge through the same processes. Our material natures form the hinge between flourishing and suffering.

Building with Integrity

I began this chapter with the aim of elucidating the relationship between materiality, flourishing and suffering in order to equip a theological response to the housing crisis. I have argued that materiality and flourishing are related through the dual sense of creaturely integrity, wherein materiality describes not only what creatures are, but also how they are created to exist. Creatures flourish through communities of activity and agency in which they become themselves, and in the process afford the possibilities for other creatures to flourish. Creatures suffer through the deformation of these material communities of creation.

It is not within the scope of this chapter to provide detailed practical proposals for changes to building practices or housing policy. Instead, to conclude this discussion, I will briefly suggest how the theological vision established in this chapter might offer a framework to underpin Christian discernment in these practical settings. This process should be one, I suggest, of discerning how to build with integrity. To build with integrity is to build homes, communities and environments that are authentic to what and how we are made to be as material creatures.

The theological account I have offered equips us to discern how our responses to suffering have the potential to deepen the very systems through which this suffering emerges. Take, for example, the renovations at Grenfell Tower. This regeneration project was intended, at face value, to meet the material needs of the most vulnerable. Yet these needs were treated as if they were separable from the broader systems through which they first arose.

It has been persuasively argued that the poor condition of Grenfell Tower was the result of chronic underspending, which then gave way to the disastrous fire of 2017. In 2013–14, the Royal Borough of Kensington and Chelsea council underspent by £30 million in an 'overachieving efficiency drive'.[32] Meanwhile, in 2013, the council put the contract for the Grenfell renovations out to tender, after an initial contractor was unable to ensure 'value for money'.[33] The projections were £1.6 million over budget. In 2014, the council secured a contract that saved them £2.5 million. Cost-cutting initiatives employed in the renovations included the use of cheaper cladding to cover the building, and opting against installing sprinkler systems, both of which would play a major role in the rapid spread of the fire. By 2017, the council had £274 million in reserves.[34]

These cost-cutting initiatives proceeded despite resident complaints concerning the council's long-term neglect of the tower, and the resulting risks to health and safety.[35] Their voices went unheard. It must not be forgotten that Grenfell

Tower primarily comprised social housing. Dependent upon this building, and the council, for accommodation, residents had little choice but to remain in an environment they knew threatened their safety, one that eventually either claimed their lives, or left them burdened with trauma and displacement.

The Grenfell Tower fire was an outworking of the systems and processes that characterize the housing crisis more broadly, which I expounded at the beginning of this chapter. The renovations were complicit in a broader cost-cutting imperative, ultimately worsening the destructive capacities of an already dangerous environment, papering over a problem – in this case with cladding – rather than addressing its deep roots. This response to suffering strips the material world of its creaturely integrity, perpetuating the falsehood that humanity somehow stands aloof from its surroundings, able to manipulate them at will for human ends.

Moreover, even if material improvements were not governed by damaging cost-cutting imperatives, responding to systemic suffering only through one-off interventions reflects an inadequate understanding of how creatures suffer and flourish in their materiality. If, as I have suggested above, systemic suffering emerges through the formation and sedimentation of habits that span whole communities of creatures, the healing of these communities cannot come through sporadic, top-down intervention.

The theological framework I have offered calls us to perceive the nature of the problem we face first by way of creaturely integrity, and in so doing it guides our understanding of how we might work towards long-term change. Our habit-making natures allow us to become bound in destructive cycles, but they are first and foremost a blessing, the particular way in which we are called to become ourselves in relation to other creatures. As such, by recognizing that materiality serves as a hinge between suffering and flourishing, we can find hope for change. Habits can be learnt and formed, but they can also be unlearnt and re-formed. Building with integrity requires cultivating practices and habits – including political and economic habits – that encourage the gradual re-formation of creaturely communities that have become deformed under human sin.

One such practice is suggested by Timothy Gorringe in his theological reflections on the built environment, namely a 'new vernacular' in building.[36] The vernacular is 'the language of ordinary people'.[37] In the context of building, a vernacular is an architecture particular to regional place and community. Building with a vernacular requires responsiveness to local climates and landscapes, their characteristic material features, and the given limits of their resources. A building vernacular might involve prioritizing the use of locally and sustainably sourced building materials, for example. This approach therefore emphasizes the interdependence of human creatures with their broader material environments, calling for greater attention to how these particular environments might flourish.

A building vernacular is also rooted in social tradition and identity, allowing individuals and communities to participate more fully in crafting life-giving homes and neighbourhoods.[38] It therefore binds together material improvement with the empowerment of those who are disempowered by systems of injustice. Such an approach might help to re-form the reductive and damaging treatment of the material world that is at the heart of systemic inequality, leading to building practices that are authentic to the integrity of creatures, and the way in which they flourish in communities of creation.

These examples illustrate how a theological vision of creaturely integrity can underpin practical discernment in the context of housing. This discernment begins with the recognition that the processes through which the housing crisis has emerged are so dangerous because they are so mundane. They are malformations of the very processes through which we are made to flourish, and thus strike at the heart of our creaturely integrity. We are creatures of habit, who become in and with the creaturely communities that afford us the time, space and conditions in which to be ourselves. In a fallen world, systems of injustice take shape through these material configurations of our lives: in our homes, schools, workplaces and neighbourhoods.

The theological account I have offered calls us to perceive

this suffering first by way of the integrity of creatureliness. Beginning with creatureliness reminds us that the basic truth about the world is the love of God that is its source and end. Meeting suffering with confidence in this love refuses it any sense of ultimacy.

Emphasizing that suffering is a malformation of creaturely integrity, however, also reminds us that none of us are outside observers of the housing crisis. Framing the housing crisis in the language of sin calls for recognition that we are implicated in, and habituated by, the systems through which this crisis has arisen. More than this, our very attempts to respond to suffering are also complexly complicit in sin. If we ignore this fact, we risk becoming blind to the ways in which our own attempts to secure justice might perpetuate the problems we protest.

Ending with this emphasis on our complicity in sin reminds us that learning to build with integrity is part of a broader process of the re-formation of our creaturely natures. Sin is only healed by Christ, whose incarnation begins our re-creation, which only God can work, but in which we are called to participate.

Only because Christ, through whom all things were created, has made his dwelling with us can we learn to dwell in the world with integrity. The Scriptures offer us a vision of salvation in which our creaturely materiality is reconfigured, gradually restored in its life-giving mutuality. Jesus is the Word made flesh, trained as a carpenter and craftsman, working miracles and healings, dismantling structures of oppressive power, and instituting the sacraments. The Spirit, meanwhile, hovers over the formless creation, gives life to Christ in Mary's womb, works in and through the material substances of the sacraments, rests on the disciples in tongues of fire, and incorporates us into Christ's body. We cannot will away sin or its effects, but we can trust that even now God – the Father, the Son, and the Holy Spirit – draws us towards the rest that the whole creation will enjoy in the creator, as it flourishes in the integrity of its creatureliness.

Notes

1 BBC (2020), 'BBC Briefing – Housing', 26 February (online), available at http://news.files.bbci.co.uk/include/newsspec/pdfs/bbc-briefing-housing-newsspec-26534.pdf (accessed 23.5.20).

2 Buck, D. and Gregory, S. (2018), *Housing and Health: Opportunities for Sustainability and Transformation Partnerships*, The King's Fund, p. 16, available at www.kingsfund.org.uk/sites/default/files/2018-03/Housing_and_health_final.pdf (accessed 23.5.20).

3 Ige, J. and colleagues (2019), 'The Relationship between Buildings and Health: A Systematic Review', *Journal of Public Health*, 41.2, pp. e121–e132.

4 Howden-Chapman, P. and colleagues (2007), 'Effect of Insulating Existing Houses on Health Inequality: Cluster Randomized Study in the Community', *British Medical Journal*, 334.7591, p. 460.

5 Pevalin, D. J. and colleagues (2017), 'The Impact of Persistent Poor Housing Conditions on Mental Health: A Longitudinal Population-based Study', *Preventive Medicine*, 105, p. 309.

6 McDade, S. and Kousoulis, A. (2020), *Tackling Social Inequalities to Reduce Mental Health Problems: How Everyone Can Flourish Equally*, London: Mental Health Foundation, pp. 17–23.

7 Pevalin and colleagues, 'The Impact', p. 309.

8 Reeves, A. and colleagues (2016), 'Reductions in the United Kingdom's Government Housing Benefit and Symptoms of Depression in Low-income Households', *American Journal of Epidemiology*, 184.6, p. 425.

9 Holding, E. and colleagues (2019), 'Exploring the Relationship Between Housing Concerns, Mental Health and Wellbeing: A Qualitative Study of Social Housing Tenants', *Journal of Public Health*, DOI: https://doi.org/10.1093/pubmed/fdz076, p. 4.

10 Holding and colleagues, 'Exploring', p. 4.

11 Elliott, I. (2016), *Poverty and Mental Health: A Review to Inform the Joseph Rowntree Foundation's Anti-poverty Strategy*, London: Mental Health Foundation, pp. 63–4.

12 Soskice, J. M. (2013), 'Creation and the glory of creatures', *Modern Theology*, 29.2, pp. 172–85, p. 173.

13 McFarland, I. (2014), *From Nothing: A Theology of Creation*, Louisville, KT: Westminster John Knox Press, p. 1.

14 The history of Christian engagement with Platonism is far more complex than can be detailed here. See May, G. (2004), *Creatio ex Nihilo: The Doctrine of 'Creation out of Nothing' in Early Christian Thought*, trans. Worrall, A. S., 2nd edn, London: T&T Clark.

15 McFarland, *From Nothing*, p. 10.

16 McFarland, *From Nothing*, p. 184.

17 Julian of Norwich (1966), *Revelations of Divine Love*, trans. Wolters, C., London: Penguin Books, p. 68.

18 Soskice, Creation, pp. 172–85, 158.

19 Augustine (1998), *Confessions*, trans. Chadwick, H., Oxford World's Classics, Oxford: Oxford University Press, pp. 61–2.

20 I borrow the concept of communities of creation from Wirzba, N. (2003), *The Paradise of God: Renewing Religion in an Ecological Age*, Oxford: Oxford University Press.

21 Augustine (2002), *On Genesis*, trans. Hill, E., ed. Rotelle, J. E., The Works of Saint Augustine, vol. 1/13, New York: New City Press, p. 174.

22 Williams, R. (2016), *On Augustine*, London: Bloomsbury Continuum, p. 94.

23 McFarland, *From Nothing*, p. 185.

24 Augustine, *On Genesis*, p. 260.

25 Augustine, *On Genesis*, p. 260.

26 This account of rest is intentionally resonant with scriptural notions of the Sabbath.

27 Theologians have not always been faithful to this implication. For the ways in which Christian anthropocentrism has been complicit in ecological damage and the suffering of indigenous communities, see Jennings, W. J. (2019), 'Reframing the World: Toward an Actual Christian Doctrine of Creation', *International Journal of Systematic Theology*, 21.4, pp. 388–407.

28 Carlisle, C. (2014), *On Habit*, London: Routledge, p. 75.

29 Anything that exists, whether animate or inanimate, is a creature. Our engagement with other creatures in building includes not only our felling of trees, but also our production of synthetic building materials.

30 How other creatures flourish or suffer in our building practices requires discernment. Do trees flourish by being part of a house, or do they suffer in being felled? Much depends upon circumstance, and our practices must always remain open to challenge as we learn more of what flourishing means for other creatures and their communities.

31 Augustine (1991), *The Trinity*, trans. Hill, E., ed. Rotelle, J. E., The Works of Saint Augustine, vol. 1/5, New York: New City Press, p. 330.

32 *The Guardian*, 2017, 'My Council Tax Rebate from Kensington and Chelsea is Blood Money', 16 June (online), available at www.theguardian.com/uk-news/2017/jun/16/my-council-tax-rebate-from-kensington-and-chelsea-is-blood-money (accessed 23.5.20).

33 Hills, J. (2017), 'Grenfell Tower: Original Proposed Contractor Was Dropped to Reduce Cost of Refurbishment Project', *ITV News*, 15 June (online), available at www.itv.com/news/2017-06-15/grenfell-tower-original-proposed-contractor-was-dropped-to-reduce-cost-of-refurbishment-project/ (accessed 23.5.20).

34 Syal, R. and Jones, H. (2017), 'Kensington and Chelsea Council has £274m in Reserves', *The Guardian*, 19 June (online), available at www.theguardian.com/uk-news/2017/jun/19/kensington-chelsea-council-has-274m-in-reserves-grenfell-tower-budget-surplus (accessed 23.7.20).

35 Grenfell Action Group (2016), 'KMCTO – Playing with fire!', *Grenfell Action Group*, 20 November, available at https://grenfellaction group.wordpress.com/2016/11/20/kctmo-playing-with-fire/ (accessed 23.5.20). See also Pasha-Robinson, L. (2017), 'Grenfell Tower Fire: MPs Attack Kensington Council for Failure to Spend £270m Reserves on Housing', *Independent*, 17 June (online), available at www.independent.co.uk/news/uk/home-news/grenfell-tower-royal-borough-kensington-chelsea-council-stockpiled-274m-despite-warnings-resi dents-a7795411.html (accessed 23.7.20).

36 Gorringe, T. J. (2002), *A Theology of the Built Environment: Justice, Empowerment, Redemption*, Cambridge: Cambridge University Press, p. 103.

37 Gorringe, *A Theology*, p. 105.

38 Gorringe, *A Theology*, pp. 92–4.

8

Good Coming from Nazareth: Challenging Housing Stigma

MIKE LONG

There is a growing consensus that the housing system is failing. The scale of the problem is manifest across Britain in the more than one million families on housing waiting lists[1] and the 320,000 people classed as homeless.[2] The reasons for this are many: the relative unaffordability of housing for purchase; the high rental values in the private rented sector; and the paucity of new housing, especially social housing. Much of this is driven by high asset prices, particularly in the south-east of England, in major cities and in popular rural locations such as coastal towns. In other words, there is not one single housing crisis but many, generated by a common dynamic but whose character has its own particularity. A chasm is developing between those in relative housing comfort and those whose housing is precarious, insecure, unsafe, overcrowded or stigmatized. While acknowledging that there are many whose experiencing of renting is positive, essentially the chasm is between two broad groups: owners and renters.

Social housing plays a vital part in the fabric of our housing provision, yet it has become the poor relation of the system. It can play an increasingly significant role in alleviating the misery that our housing crisis causes. The Church has made, and continues to make, an important contribution in this field: as a provider of social housing (often through housing associations); as the repository of a vision of how people belong in communities and how these may flourish and thrive; and as advocate for the poor and vulnerable, and their empowerment for greater agency in relation to their housing.

The Church has a long history of providing accommodation to those in need, starting with acts of individual hospitality in the early Church, to the hospitality of monasteries, the provision of almshouses, and Church-sponsored housing programmes and associations. In other words, the Church has a firm basis of engagement upon which to develop further reflection.

Christian theology brings the perspective that human beings belong together, find their fulfilment through relationships with one another, and that salvation is worked out in company with others. It is deeply personal, but not individual. Hence issues of housing can never be reduced to technical considerations of architecture, design or planning alone. The critical question to ask is not so much 'what kind of housing do we need?' but 'what kind of communities can be established to foster human flourishing?' As we shall see, the biblical concept of 'house' is as much about people and communities as it is about physical dwellings.

Housing matters because it has a fundamental impact on human wellbeing. There is a tension inherent in the call of God's people to a pilgrim way of life, a nomadic discipleship following Christ, and spurning the attractions of security and stability. Yet disciples and itinerant apostles relied upon on the hospitality of others; indeed, the early Church depended on house fellowship – and in later centuries on the monastic communities. Jesus warned against a preoccupation with earthly satisfactions (Matt. 6.25–34), but his teaching was not an indictment of a settled lifestyle – rather, the dangers of wealth, comfort and self-interest.[3] Any theological contribution to the issue of social housing needs to address the question: 'what is the Christian vision of life "in all its fullness"?' And what role does housing play in this?

In considering fullness of life, we need to think not merely of individuals or households in isolation, but of the kind of communities that housing creates. Owner-occupier areas tend to promote people with similar interests, backgrounds and income levels. By contrast, social housing can enhance mixed developments, particularly in inner-city areas otherwise inaccessible to all but the most wealthy. The assertion that 'the earth belongs to the Lord' (Ps. 24.1) means that ownership of land is therefore contingent on God's sovereign rule rather than legal title, and cannot be reduced to matters of market value alone. Unlike material commodities, it does not deteriorate with use or the passage of time. However, neither this premise nor a right-based approach are best placed to offer theological reflection on social housing. We need instead to consider the kind of life that is encouraged or impaired by the nature of one's accommodation in engagement with the gospel witness. There are several themes to address: how a sense of 'home' enables human fulfilment and fosters community, and how the residents may feel more empowered with regard to their housing.

Jesus asserted the importance of having one's own home: he condemned those who exploited others' vulnerabilities, citing the 'devouring of widows' houses' (Luke 20.45–47), echoing the prophet Micah (Micah 2.2). It is the locus for much of Jesus' ministry: he visited people in their homes, accepted hospitality, and taught and performed healings there. In the parable of the Prodigal Son (Luke 15.11–32) the celebration at the family home is given as an illustration of the merciful welcome that the father gives to the 'prodigal'. The use of home as a metaphor for the realm of God's sovereign rule is also found in John 14.1–6. Here Jesus speaks of the promises of God to faithful disciples in terms of a many-roomed divine dwelling, in which there is space for all. Such a sense of one's own space – unconfined, unrestricted and secure – affords the physical and emotional room for one to grow, develop, and fulfil one's potential.

In this respect it is significant that the name 'Jesus' itself contains helpful connotations here. Jesus, 'one who saves', is the equivalent of the Hebrew Joshua and is derived from the Aramaic *Yeshua*. Its Hebrew root lies in the verb *yasha*, to save, and whose original meaning is to be wide or spacious, as it still does today in Arabic.[4] There is an etymological connection between the concept of salvation and the one who brings

131

it, and the sense of being unconfined, unconstrained, liberated. One aspect of the salvation that Christ brings might therefore embrace a sense of physical or mental space through which we might have a greater sense of human flourishing. Christ himself performed this role: when he challenged conventional attitudes, when he socialized with those considered undesirable company, when he healed untouchables and foreigners, and when he charged his followers with a mission beyond the confines of Israel. The Church's role in offering his gospel of salvation may be called to offer physical space, but also the mental room that offers sanctuary and hospitality as well as prayer.

It is in this light that Jesus' words about the 'Father's house' comprising many rooms (*monai*) are given fresh significance. *Monai* is the word for stopping-places, inns or temporary halts. Much has been written about the meaning of 'Father's house', and in particular whether Jesus was referring to something earthly or heavenly. The important point here should be what this dwelling-place enables, rather than what it constitutes. Furthermore, there is added significance in the use of 'many' through which we find a resonance with the spatial aspects of salvation. The purpose of Jesus' words, in addition to providing reassurance to apprehensive disciples, was to assure them that in God's house (earthly or heavenly) there is breadth that exudes welcome, hospitality and mercy. The 'house' (or household of God, perhaps) is more a 'social metaphor' than a spatial one,[5] but the former does not preclude a sense of the latter. The ideal 'home', it would seem, is a reflection of the kingdom of God, and 'to receive God's justice is to receive access to home'.[6]

Housing and shelter are vital aspects for human wellbeing, but the key issue is the capacity to establish and sustain home. Elements of this include a sense of security, acceptance, belonging, safety, physical and emotional privacy, and the ability to foster a sense of personal or family identity. A home is far more than accommodation; residing in a barracks, school dormitory, hospital ward, prison cell or hotel does not provide these goods, despite the security and welfare each provide. A home environment is key in its contribution to human wellbeing and flourishing, consonant with the scriptural vision of the blessed life, in which each person shall dwell under 'his' own vine and fig-tree (Micah 4.4), undisturbed, with the sense of security and freedom from intrusion or molestation being critical to the good life.

Any consideration of home does however need to acknowledge its deeply contextual aspect. Concepts such as personal space and individual expression are neither universal nor valued equally. The very conditions that for some will bring comfort and security are ones that others may find oppressive or intimidating. The concept of home must therefore be detached from any sense that the normative is a Western, individualist, nuclear-family, 'private' home.

The work for house, *oikos*, is used commonly in both the New Testament and the Septuagint. It can refer not only to physical dwellings but to the wider household, as well as figuratively (the 'house of David'). The household was commonly the locus of family, economic and communal life.[7] For many cultures, and for much of Western history, 'home' is located within a wider network of kinship and clan identities and settlements. In industrial, urbanized societies the household has been replaced with notions of 'home' as the primary unit of family and individual nurture, with all the concomitant associations of privacy and freedom. In giving due consideration to an unromanticized theology of 'home', therefore, we must connect this to the theme of community. Theologically, we need to locate our reflections on *oikos* within the context of *ekklesia*, the community that sustains Christian life and faith.

Such a community is characterized by interdependence and mutuality, through which the nurture of the individual and the community are ensured. A clear expression of this is found in the distribution of spiritual gifts in 1 Corinthians 12, where difference and togetherness cohere. The sense of 'distribution' does not imply a haphazard scattering of gifts across the various members, but a deliberate allocation of diverse gifts in ways appropriate to the recipient. This is analogous to taxonomic classification, in which different species are arranged according to both sameness and difference: they belong to the same family of shared characteristics and yet also exhibit distinctive traits that enable flourishing to occur in a particular environment.[8] Diversity is both rooted in, and emerges from, a certain unity. Gifts are given to each equally but differently, and are given to the whole, for the flourishing of all.

Another way of describing the way that the individual and collective work in harmony is Jeremy Begbie's description of the evocative singing of freedom songs in South Africa. He writes of how voices combine to reinforce each other, without dominating or constraining others:

> It is a space not of a hundred voices each with their mutually exclusive and bounded 'place', but a space of overlapping sounds, an uncrowded, expansive space without 'edges' where distinct voices mutually establish each other.[9]

A sense of community is thus vital for a dwelling to be truly 'home', and this sense is weakened by insecurity. Tenants are unlikely to invest time and labour in their communities if they do not have a sense of belonging – for instance, through the fear they may have to leave at short notice. By contrast, secure tenants may, for example, decorate communal areas with flowers and garden plants in the knowledge that it is not a wasted effort, and thus improve the quality of the neighbourhood for all.

Social housing is a public good. Without it, many people on lower incomes could not afford to live in the inner cities, or places where they can commute to work easily. Longer and more expensive travel would make it harder for many businesses to find the staff they need, and there would be wage inflationary pressures on those they do employ, with consequent implications for the wider economy. Social housing also helps to provide social diversification and to build stronger, more resilient communities. This may sound strange to those whose image of social housing is large, often prefabricated estates on the edges of cities. Much social housing is in fact located in mixed areas, partly through the introduction of Right to Buy in 1981 (when council housing stock was sold at discounted prices to tenants), but also through newer smaller-scale developments. In some parts of London multi-million pound house owners live immediately adjacent to neighbours in social housing, and many expensive houses in the area remain seldom used. The contrast is stark, but not so stark as if it were comprised of physically separated dwellings, such as in gated communities.

Another of the ways in which a dwelling's ability to act as a home is impaired is through stigma. Sadly, many social housing residents report high levels of public stigma simply because of the kind of housing they live in[10] and many studies have described the damaging impact it has on wellbeing. Residents have described feeling angry, hurt and upset, and made to feel like 'second-class citizens'.[11] They experience embarrassment and shame, and the normal pleasure one gets from having a new home is reduced. The effects of stigma impact every area of life, so that it can become a significant blight on one's interior and exterior life: on self-confidence, relationships (particularly with family or friends living elsewhere), employment opportunities, financial services and much more.

A common question on meeting someone new is to ask where they live. This may reflect simple curiosity but for those already experiencing such stigma it can contribute to an assumption about the impression being inferred, that a less favourable picture of the respondent is being made. Surveys of residents have indicated that, on some housing estates, residents feel that they are treated less favourably by many agencies including the police, estate agents, taxi firms (leading residents to give false addresses), as well as being portrayed unfairly in the media more generally.

It is hard to find direct evidence of stigma on the part of organizations, not least because it is often expressed in subtle ways. Few employers will admit to discrimination, yet they are more willing to concede that they know of others who may well adopt such practices.[12] As one study concludes:

the weight of evidence, coupled with some known indiscretions by, e.g., employers and surveyors, suggests that the residents' perceptions of prejudice by such institutions are likely to be grounded in at least partial reality.[13]

One key finding of recent research has been that stigmatizing attitudes to social housing residents were significantly higher among those with less experience of the actual housing estate than those with greater knowledge or experience.[14] Those with a deep level of knowledge, such as local residents and employees, tended to have a less pathological attitude than those living further away, or professionals based elsewhere. Such explanations are more dominant in the media, in wider society and in academia, despite other ones based on inequality or a complex combination of factors and forces. One persistent myth is that BAME groups constitute a disproportionate number of social housing allocations, one that the English Housing Survey 2015–16 clearly indicated was false.[15] Because the sources of housing stigma lie with such a wide multitude of people and agencies, a strategy that focuses narrowly faces significant difficulties.[16]

Such false narratives can be hard to shift and require a multi-faceted approach that covers objective data and subjective experiences. An illustration may be helpful here. A Commission on Social Housing was established by the charity Shelter in 2018.[17] One of its key activities was a series of 'citizen jury'-type events in various locations across England, led by a market research think tank and requiring commissioners to listen, but not otherwise engage. At one such gathering a frequent refrain was racist allegations about those who were being offered new tenancies. At the lunch break one of the commissioners, who happened to be the chief executive of the local authority in which the meeting was taking place, obtained the statistics on housing allocation by ethnicity. When she presented figures showing that the proportion of allocations to BAME members was lower than the percentage of BAME residents within that authority, the response was disbelief and rejection. She was not believed, either because it was convenient to do so, or because the authority she represented was not trusted. The way such misconceptions can be challenged successfully is through personal experience – and this has implications for how the Church can act to remedy the negative images that many experience with regard to social housing.

It is noteworthy that we have one instance recorded in Scripture where Jesus experienced the stigma attached to his social origins – at least among those in Judaea – as witnessed by Nathaniel's question, 'Can anything good come out of Nazareth?' (John 1.46). This remark is variously interpreted in terms of its degree of denigration of Jesus' home town, but it is unquestionably a comment that is at best a slur, an uncomplimentary piece of snobbery. Its very preservation in the Gospel account is significant in itself, and may echo a development in which the term 'Nazarene' was used pejoratively,[18] and which centuries later the Church of the Nazarene adopted as a synonym for those who experience marginalization and stigma.[19] From the Lukan account of his birth in a stable, to the company he ministered among, to the crucifixion, Christ's incarnation embraces an identification with the stigmatized, with those whose insights and perspectives are dismissed by those with more influence and power.

Stigma also affects relations between tenants and landlords. Social housing tenants describe feeling devalued when registering concerns or complaints, and the Shelter Commission report on social housing expressed the firm opinion that social housing should be for all who wish it, not just for some. It advocated 'tenure-blind' developments where the type of occupancy is not visible from the outside appearance of the property, in contrast to recent developments in which separate 'poor doors' are designed for social housing tenants in mixed developments.[20] The furore over the Lilian Baylis estate in London in 2019 provides a good illustration of such segregated development: the developer erected a wall to prevent social housing families accessing a communal area, thus making it exclusively for leaseholders.[21] Following widespread public condemnation, the dividing wall was removed.

The housing crisis is largely a product of shortage of supply, in which social housing has withered on the vine. It is helpful therefore to trace a brief history in order to understand why

tenant empowerment, including strengthening tenant voice,
is so important. The function of social housing has changed
tremendously since its inception over a century ago. It was
introduced to improve conditions for urban working-class
tenants as private renting was expensive, insecure, overcrowded
and could not deliver decent, affordable housing for local
people. The first introduction of council-funded housing was
in 1869 in Vauxhall, Liverpool, following legislation that
allowed municipalities to borrow at subsidized rates from
government.[22] Initiatives were also taken by Victorian phil-
anthropists such as Octavia Hill and the Peabody Trust, who
constructed homes for the local working classes, but in time
often ran into financial difficulties. By the early years of the
twentieth century a plethora of local authority schemes were
being tried in inner cities, suburbs and rural areas. Between the
wars the cities grew enormously as new suburbs were created,
and a further housing boom began in the late 1940s as a wave
of new towns emerged, and Labour and Conservative governments vied with one another to build the greatest number of
council homes. Such housing was intended for the ordinary
working family and many people took pride in obtaining their
first tenancy. Social housing was now designed for the general
population rather than a particular social class, and aspired
to Bevan's much quoted vision of housing where 'the doctor,
the grocer, the butcher and the . . . labourer all lived in the
same street'.[23] In other words, a mixed community. From the
late 1950s the changing nature of housing need, with falling
household sizes as well as for aesthetic reasons, led to the construction of high-rise flats and the use of prefabricated concrete
systems. Innovative designs featuring 'cities in the sky' with
elaborate walkways became common features, but in many
cases became notorious for poor amenities, design flaws, crime
and antisocial behaviour. During this postwar period many
churches became involved in setting up housing associations,
involving small-scale developments on ecclesiastical land or
purchasing run-down properties to renovate for letting. Economic pressures such as access to loans for development or
refurbishment, as well as economies of scale, have forced many

housing associations to merge in recent decades. In so doing, some of the larger organizations have been criticized for losing sight of their initial *raison d'être*.

A significant policy shift took place in the 1980s when many council homes were bought by their tenants, and a significant proportion subsequently let for profit. Since the 1990s much of the remaining council housing stock has been offloaded on to a plethora of bodies to manage such properties.[24] A steady increase in home ownership over many decades peaked in 2003 but has declined since, accompanied by a significant expansion in the private rental sector (PRS).[25]

A tragic watershed in housing was the June 2017 Grenfell Tower fire in west London that claimed 72 lives. A common refrain in the fire's aftermath was the experience of being ignored by those responsible for tenants' welfare and safety. Many tenants there spoke of feeling ignored, demeaned and stigmatized simply as a result of where they lived. Concerns about safety and maintenance issues were too often responded to in ways that made tenants acutely aware of their own power-lessness. Many social tenants continue to feel happy and secure in their properties, but the experiences at Grenfell elicited a disturbing resonance from many.

The key factor that has had most impact on social housing has been residualization, the process whereby – through scarcity of housing provision – properties that are available are prioritized for those in greatest need. There are many causes of this, including the dramatic slowdown in new social housing construction and the effect of Right To Buy, where councils were unable to replace the stock that tenants purchased. Positive legislation such as the Race Relations Act (1976) and the Housing Homelessness Act (1977) removed barriers to housing access and hence demand increased.[26] In contrast to earlier intentions of creating mixed communities, social housing has become, in many instances, the housing of last resort. The consequence of this shift has been a much higher concentration of tenants with (often) significant problems such as poor mental health, weak support structures, and substance abuse. This has in turn prompted the labelling of 'sink estates', which reinforces poor images of those who live there. Residualization has been more accidental than by design, but its impact is indisputable. The solution is to increase capacity: to build or renovate more homes for use. This is not confined to social housing, for the condition of the private rental sector has a direct bearing. Indeed, as was stated above, the Victorian impetus for much social housing was the inability of the private rental sector to provide affordable accommodation for a local population, and in many parts of England today this is also the case. Scarcity of housing pushes up asset prices and rental values and makes it harder for local authorities to require developers to ensure much social housing provision.[27]

Social housing providers in urban areas with high land values are in an unenviable position. Gentrification has taken place in many parts of London and some other cities, with many large (and on occasion, iconic) estates sold by local authorities and demolished, tenants being relocated to distant areas, or even other cities.[28] Social housing providers there can be faced with the dilemma of maintaining old, costly buildings worth many millions of pounds, or alternatively capitalizing on the asset through sale, and in its place purchasing newer, more easily maintained properties – but in less popular, distant locations. Tenants may thus experience a process of gentrification even from local housing associations. They may also prefer to stay in overcrowded accommodation – due to the high value they place on remaining in the local community, with its estab-lished network of relationships, schooling and access to work – rather than apply for better housing in better, but less con-venient locations. To some this may sound little different from choices made by owner-occupiers or those who rent privately, but there is an important difference: those in social housing have far less choice in where they live, and often the net value to social housing tenants is higher, because their need of local support systems may be greater (peer support, childminding, etc.) than those on higher incomes in the same neighbourhood.

The challenges of our housing crisis require responses at every level from national and local policy, to the detail of com-munity plans, to structures that empower tenants. One aspect of the need for empowerment is the challenging of housing stigma at every level. As with other forms of unfair discrimination, the precursor to solutions is the acknowledgement of the experience and the desire to understand its dynamics.

Social housing tenants have often been treated (unfairly) as the recipients of welfare, and not as persons with agency of their own. Measures that improve tenants' own sense of self-worth and dignity are clearly vital aspects of any good housing policy. Listening to tenants requires a clear and robust framework, and a willingness to adapt on the part of social landlords, for it is all too easy to be seduced into thinking that one is listening attentively, but in reality only to that which accords with what is expected or deemed acceptable. At the National Commemoration Service for the victims and survivors of the Grenfell Tower fire, held at St Paul's Cathedral, the Right Reverend Graham Tomlin concluded his sermon with a call for those in authority to find a new way 'to listen and to love'. This requires not a little humility on the part of those with power, and a readiness to consider uncomfortable truths about the ways in which people can feel stigmatized in systems that fail those they are designed to serve. Such a readiness to listen and love is reminiscent of Bonhoeffer's 'view from below' in which the world is viewed with 'incomparable value' through the lens of the marginalized and the powerless.[29] Only in such a way will tenant participation be regarded as a valuable contribution and not a token gesture.

It is with this perspective that we read Jesus' words in the parable of the rich man and Lazarus (Luke 16.19–31). Here a chasm is depicted between them that persists not only in life but in death, and one that the parable infers can only be overcome by obedience to God's message in Jesus. In true parabolic form, the chasm between the men is stark and extreme: the rich man wears purple (extremely expensive in antiquity) and feasts daily; Lazarus is malnourished and diseased. In death the division persists for Lazarus receives no burial. The rich man's failing was not his wealth per se, but his inability to see Lazarus other than as anything but ancillary to his own needs and desires. (Even the dogs attend to Lazarus!) Lazarus' own life, condition and experience are not of interest: his role in life and death is to be at the service of the rich man, and even the experience of Hades does not change this outlook. An urgent conversion here is demanded, one that embraces a new way of seeing, understanding and valuing as well as acting.

One significant obstacle to this process is complacency. Policy makers may be committed to the needs of local residents, and yet find that tenants do not feel they are being listened to sufficiently. A deeper kind of listening is therefore called for, as Tomlin mentioned, and one that continues to explore the underlying narratives among those who feel marginalized. That is not to give credence to every local conspiracy theory, but it is to recognize the forces that generate them or create mistrust in authority and management structures.

There needs to be the acknowledgement that all our institutions and programmes, however well intentioned, are not without sin. All our systems and methods of organization require recalibrating according to the needs of the people they seek to serve. The key issue in doing so – and many organizations routinely engage in obtaining feedback from their clients – is how to filter and weight the responses in order that truth might emerge. Too many consultation exercises are hindered from the outset either by popular mistrust or inadequate attention to local context. Similarly, poverty, overcrowding and desperation are often masked from view inadvertently, and to see clearly requires not only determination but openness of heart and mind.

Tenants' sense of being marginalized due to their social tenancy is linked to the sense of powerlessness. This was manifest in the wake of the Grenfell Tower fire, where local residents spoke of safety concerns going unheeded, and a 'culture of neglect'. At the heart of this matter is the imbalance of power between social tenants and their landlords (or the organizations they establish to maintain estates). Private renters may also experience this, and there is growing attention to the problem of 'trapped renters' unable to find alternative accommodation, and fearful of eviction if they complain. In addition to addressing the paucity of housing supply, strengthening tenants' rights and enhancing tenant voice are positive means of addressing the power inequities. The Church has a role in advocating these in the public sphere as well as encouraging best practices for tenant involvement and empowerment in housing associations where they have influence.

Housing policy has been shaped by economic forces, and it is clear that the market plays a vital part in the provision and distribution of varieties of housing from ownership to the private rented sector. However, housing issues cannot be reduced merely to a discussion on the appropriate distribution of commodities, for at the heart of the issue are those conditions that make for, or impair, human flourishing. Therefore, what is important for long-term social housing policy are not only the economic considerations, but a rationale that goes beyond the economic realm. Ethical and economic considerations are intertwined here but, as with other public goods, interventions and boundaries are needed to prevent a housing system being skewed towards the wealthy and powerful – with consequences for the whole of society. A strong and expanded social housing sector might serve to encourage higher standards in private renting, but need not harm private ownership.

We need more housing of all kinds, and this will serve to improve the bargaining power of the weakest and most vulnerable. A greater public consciousness of the social and economic damage that the housing crisis is inflicting is called for, and how local communities, councils and partnerships can make a difference. Most of all we need more social housing – but the key issue of all concerns the kind of communities we want to be: diverse, plural, strong, participatory communities. We have a rich tradition to draw on to inform us: our understanding of home and neighbourhood, of communities of interdependence and mutuality.

During the early period of exile in Babylon all the Israelites there were instructed to build homes, settle down, establish patterns of family life and 'seek the welfare of the city . . . for in its welfare you will find your welfare' (Jer. 29.7). Social housing should be guided similarly, that its increase in size and regulation might benefit not just those in greatest housing need, but society as a whole, today and for future generations.

Notes

1 *The Guardian*, 9 June 2018.
2 www.bbc.co.uk/news/education-46289259.
3 Gorringe, T. J. (2002), *A Theology of the Built Environment*, Cambridge: Cambridge University Press, p. 88.
4 Abarim Publications Theological Dictionary, www.abarim-publications.com/Dictionary/y/y-si-ay.html.
5 Jerome, H. and Neyrey, S. J. (2002), 'Spaces and Places, Whence and Whither, Homes and Rooms: "Territoriality" in the Fourth Gospel', *Biblical Theology Bulletin*, 32, pp. 60–75.
6 Meeks, D. (1989), *God the Economist*, Minneapolis, MI: Fortress, p. 36.
7 Meeks, *God*, p. 33; Elliott, J. H. (1981), *A Home for the Homeless*, London: SCM Press, pp. 182–200.
8 I am grateful to Professor Judith Lieu at Cambridge University for this insight and illustration.
9 Begbie, J. (2000), 'Through Music: Sound Mix', in Begbie, J., ed., *Beholding the Glory: Incarnation through the Arts*, London: Darton, Longman and Todd, pp. 151–2.
10 Over half of social renters say they are portrayed unfairly. Shelter (2019), *Building for Our Future, a Vision for Social Housing*, pp. 39–40.
11 Dean, J. and Hastings, A. (2000), *Challenging Images: Housing Estates, Stigma and Regeneration*, Bristol University: Policy Press and Joseph Rowntree Foundation, p. 21.
12 Hastings, A. (2004), 'Stigma and Social Housing Estates: Beyond Pathological Explanations', *Journal of Housing and the Built Environment*, 19.
13 Dean and Hastings, *Challenging Images*, p. 22.
14 Hastings, 'Stigma', p. 247.
15 Power, A. and Provan, B. (2018), *Overcoming the Stigma of Social Housing: Can Social Housing Rebuild its Reputation?*, London School of Economics and Political Science: Centre for Analysis of Social Exclusion.
16 Hastings, 'Stigma', p. 253.
17 Shelter, *Building*.
18 As may have been the case with Tertullus' accusation in Acts 24.5.
19 This is according to Hastings, J. (1908), *Dictionary of Christ and the Gospels*.
20 Shelter, *Building*, p. 135.
21 'London Bans Segregated Play Spaces at all New Housing Sites' (2019), *The Guardian*, 20 July.
22 Boughton, J. (2018), *Municipal Dreams*, New York: Verso, p. 13.

A helpful summary of social housing may also be found in chapters by Francis, A., Gardiner, S. and Horton, C., in Francis, A., ed. (2016), *Foxes Have Holes: Christian Reflections on Britain's Housing Need*, London: Ekklesia.

23 Power and Provan, *Overcoming*, p. 9.

24 These include Tenant Management Organisations (TMOs), Arms Length Management Organizations (ALMOs) and Housing Associations.

25 Shelter, *Building*, p. 49.

26 Power and Provan, *Overcoming*.

27 Known as Section 106 (of the 1990 Town and Country Planning Act), this allows local authorities to require developers to commit a proportion of new homes for affordable housing, but there are exemptions (Shelter, *Building*, p. 125).

28 Minton, A. (2017), *Big Capital*, London: Penguin.

29 Bonhoeffer, D. (1971), *Letters and Papers from Prison*, London: SCM Press, p. 17.

9

Room for Friendship: Building Counter-cultural Community Among Women Experiencing Addiction – in Conversation with L'Arche

FLORENCE O'TAYLOR

Introduction

Writing from home during the Covid-19-induced lockdown, The Archbishop of Canterbury's Commission on Housing, Church and Community seems particularly prescient. In a week, we have seen that some seemingly impossible things are, in fact, achievable: governments, local and national, have aimed to house everyone who is sleeping rough; a national food distribution system has been set up to protect the most vulnerable; people are largely keeping their distance in public and even getting to know their neighbours. Yet simultaneously: many families in scandalously inappropriate temporary accommodation are now unable to escape for work and play; victims of domestic violence around the country are locked in with their abusers; and the domestic killing of women has risen to more than double the average rate.[1] As we are all asked to stay home during the pandemic – and rightly so – there is no escaping the current housing crisis and inequity present in our housing system. Our home lives have become our whole lives, and when there are those without appropriate or safe places to live, the ever-present crisis has become starkly accentuated. As Jesus says in Matthew 25.40: 'Whatever you did for one of the least of these, you did for me', it is to the most vulnerable that the Church should pay attention. Imagining a just recovery from Covid-19, how therefore might the Church be at the centre of offering a prophetic approach to housing that promotes human flourishing and belonging, particularly for those on the margins of society?

One demographic whose housing needs are particularly exposed during lockdown specifically, and the housing crisis generally, is women experiencing addiction. Insecure – or lack of – housing can be a contributing factor in both the emergence of substance misuse and a barrier to recovery from it. Despite widespread acknowledgement of this, those with addiction continue to face many barriers to housing. With less provision for women experiencing addiction than men, and the relationship between domestic violence and addiction, the female population is particularly vulnerable to poor housing provision. Responding to this reality, this chapter focuses on the need for appropriate housing provision for women experiencing addiction, seeking also to build more general principles for an approach to housing that promotes human flourishing. Alongside L'Arche, we will look at the work of Professor Stephanie Covington, a clinical psychologist based at the Center for Gender and Justice in the USA, who has developed a holistic recovery model – Women's Integrated Treatment (WIT) – that centralizes the need for safety and spirituality for recovery. Notably, a safe environment is difficult to achieve when you are either without stable – or any – housing.

Secure housing is crucial for both the prevention of and recovery from addiction among women. Addiction and homelessness are often intricately connected: substance dependence increases the risk of homelessness, and precarious accommodation – whether homeless, insecure or unsafe – increases the risk of substance misuse. Concurrently, any response that has a chance of effectively tackling such an insidious challenge must consider housing and addiction together.

Covington's approach resonates with L'Arche's relational model, and its emphasis on the human dignity of each individual as a child of God with gifts to offer. L'Arche is a federation of 149 residential communities across 38 countries where people with and without learning disabilities live together in a way that offers a potentially transformative model of accommodation for women experiencing addiction. It describes its mission as 'to make known the gifts of people with intellectual disabilities, working together toward a more human society', with mutual relationships and trust in God as the heart of the journey. We shall explore what the Church might learn from L'Arche to create good housing, community and human flourishing. The proposals are twofold; first we shall explore how the Church might respond to the current housing crisis through supporting and housing women experiencing addiction alongside women who are not (notably, those who are young, experiencing their own form of housing crisis). We will proceed by learning from the theology and spirituality of L'Arche in dialogue with contemporary gender-responsive, trauma-informed addiction research. Second, learning from L'Arche's mission to build a more just society, we shall seek to glean theological principles for good housing that build on the themes of mutuality and belonging.

The suggestions will be ambitious but also quite simple. Both will plunge into the complicated socio-political realities of addiction, trauma and homelessness, and rest in the simplicity of the Church's call to 'love our neighbour as ourselves' and exhibit Christian friendship.

A Note on Jean Vanier and L'Arche

Alongside Covid-19, I am also writing this chapter months after it has been revealed that Jean Vanier, the founder of L'Arche, has been proven to have sexually abused at least six women in the context of spiritual accompaniment during his time leading the community. I proposed to write about how the wisdom of L'Arche could speak into the current housing crisis before these revelations that Jean Vanier was an abuser came to pass. I conceived of his theology as both pastoral and political; capable, as Hauerwas attested, of transforming both

148

individuals and communities into people of peace.[2] And I had long venerated Vanier, alongside many others, as a man who truly lived the theology he espoused. I was wrong. The news of his abuse of six women reveals, as the L'Arche report states, that in both his life and his theology there was a coercive underside. It is crucial that the experience of the women he abused is not minimized, nor conciliatory narratives accepted, but the grievous nature of his sexual abuse taken seriously. It is clear that L'Arche and Vanier are not synonymous; however, there is a reality that Vanier has held an integral role in both the founding and development of the community. In Vanier abusing women, the founding story of L'Arche has been shattered.

As someone who has spent her career thus far in the women's sector, working with survivors of domestic violence and sexual abuse, I have wrestled with whether to write this chapter at all. It was immediately clear that to use any of Vanier's writing would be inappropriate and dangerous, and I am grateful for the counsel I have received in how or whether to proceed. I believe that while the sin and sinner must not be separated, following the wise insights of Jane Barter and Irene Tuffrey-Wijne among others, there is a 'distinction to be made between the founder and the community that he helped found'.[3] This has been supported by members of L'Arche I have spoken with, who are firm in the belief that while for those outside the movement L'Arche and Vanier are almost synonymous, within it Vanier played a less central role in forming contemporary communities' identities. L'Arche International has been unequivocal in condemning the actions of its founder and describing Vanier's actions as 'incompatible with the basic rules of respect and dignity of persons, and contrary to the fundamental principles on which L'Arche is based'.[4] It commended the courage of the women affected, both those who spoke up and 'any others who may not have spoken up', before asking for 'forgiveness for these events which took place in the context of L'Arche'.[5] Most importantly, I feel able to proceed because each of the abused women named in their motivation for coming forward against Jean Vanier, a desire to 'help L'Arche to reflect on the past and to avoid any similar events in the future'.[6]

They seem to be comfortable to work with the organization, and so I feel comfortable to do the same here in drawing on L'Arche's theology and spirituality. I will not draw on any writings of Jean Vanier in this chapter, recognizing extensive work is needed to consider how and whether to re-engage with his work in the future. Rather, I will explore other voices in and akin to L'Arche, including John Swinton and Samuel Wells, to explore the rich themes of friendship and mutuality and how they might support a response to the housing crisis facing women experiencing addiction that promotes community and human flourishing.

Understanding Women's Experience of Addiction and the Housing Crisis

The housing crisis is acutely felt by the growing number of women experiencing addiction, with safe accommodation for these women both difficult to access and underfunded.[7] This contributes to a growing crisis of epic proportions: in 2018, 1,375 women died from drug poisoning in England and Wales, with around two-thirds of deaths due to substance misuse. The death toll has increased for nine consecutive years and is the highest number of drug-related deaths since records began.[8] Addiction specialists are decrying this as a public health emergency, prompting calls for damaging cuts to treatment services to be urgently reversed.[9]

Housing is crucial for recovery from addiction for women due to the correlation between trauma and addiction. Despite this, women experiencing addiction are one of the most precariously housed demographics in the country, with a lack of residential rehabilitation and barriers to accessing rental accommodation. This is, in part, due to a lack of gender-based research that recognizes the particular experience of women, and a subsequent lack of appropriate provision. Historically, substance abuse treatment has developed as a single-focused intervention based on the needs of addicted men, ignoring the key correlation between trauma and addiction for women. In fact, the United Nations commissioned *Promoting a Gender-responsive Approach to Addiction*[10] recognizing that most addiction programmes are 'ineffective on women' because they ignore exactly this. Despite well-evidenced links between gender-based violence and substance dependence among women, with substance abuse used to cope with the trauma associated with violence, safe accommodation for women is kept behind high barriers and remains under-resourced.[11]

It is in a particular macro socio-economic context that women find themselves facing addiction and homelessness. The complex relationships between domestic violence, trauma, addiction and homelessness are clear, and the need apparent for safety, support and secure housing in recovery. Addiction and homelessness are not spontaneous experiences, but intimately connected to the relational, environmental and socio-political aspects of a woman's life. A generation of public policy that has systemically underinvested in our housing stock, particularly affordable and social housing, has resulted in a housing crisis that particularly affects those on low income and in need of support. Women experiencing addiction try to find housing in this context. The Right to Buy scheme combined with an introduction of housing benefits that can be paid to private landlords has increased the percentage of private tenancies, which are less secure than social housing equivalents. Government investment in social housing has halved since 1980, housing benefit payments have been stagnant since 2013, and the social housing stock is around one-third of the level it was 40 years ago.[12] This has left one million families on the waiting list, many of whom find themselves in overcrowded, unsuitable temporary accommodation such as office blocks converted into studio apartments housing whole families.[13] The shortages are so serious that councils are struggling to find even temporary accommodation for many. According to Crisis, 18,000 fewer social lets were made to homeless households in 2017–18 than in 2007–08, despite the substantial rise in statutory homelessness in that decade.[14] The precarity of housing that women with addictions are facing is not inevitable, but in part due to policy choices that have not prioritized those on the margins of society.

Yet, as we have noted, secure housing is crucial for both the prevention of and recovery from addiction among women. The relationship between domestic violence and addiction is well documented, and therefore safety – including housing – plays a crucial role in recovery. There is an endemic lack of provision for women experiencing homelessness, with few local authorities having the services in place that respond collectively to women's multiple disadvantage, experience of addiction and homelessness. According to Solace Women's Aid, '30 per cent of women seeking shelter are turned away six or more times' and '53 per cent of women lose their secure tenancy after fleeing abuse'.[15] Combined with cuts to drug and alcohol provision funding, there is an increasingly dire need to house and support women experiencing addiction. This is corroborated by Covington's centralization of safety as one of the key elements in recovery, prioritizing caring for the individual in the present and creating a safe place for them, which will often require a women-only space with a supportive environment.

WIT is one model that has proven successful among women experiencing addiction. Covington is adamant that addiction must be understood from a systems perspective and a holistic model of recovery is essential for women, and she employs Trauma Theory in her approach. She defines trauma as 'both an event and a particular response to an event' and describes Post Traumatic Stress Disorder (PTSD) as a 'disease of disconnection'.[16] Describing the journey of addiction as a downward spiral, where women's lives increasingly wind more tightly around the addictive substance, she frames the recovery process as the opposing upward spiral. In this upward spiral, she depicts how, in recovery, the woman's life will still revolve around the drug, but in increasingly expanded circles away from addiction into a fuller existence, where a healthier form of self can develop, with relationships and spiritual life transformed. She posits that any approach will be ineffective unless it acknowledges the correlation between violence, abuse and addiction, and the weight that trauma can impact on women's lives. It is increasingly recognized that many women who relapse in recovery and have previously been considered treatment failures are trauma survivors who used substances to medicate. Her holistic approach integrates trauma services into her recovery model, meeting the aforementioned need for provision that recognizes the multiple complex needs of women experiencing addiction and facing homelessness. This holistic approach resonates with L'Arche's relational model, and its emphasis on the human dignity of each individual as a child of God with gifts to offer. No one-size-fits-all policy will be appropriate for every individual facing such complex challenges, and funding for a myriad of flexible, person-centred approaches is what is required.[17] In conversation with leading addiction research, the Church might build communities inspired by L'Arche and enriched by its core values to effectively support and be with women experiencing addiction. A residential community of women with and without addictions that creates a safe space, while offering specialist support along the lines of WIT, is one holistic response to the current crisis that would serve as a preventative and rehabilitative approach to both homelessness and addiction in the female population.

There is also insurmountable evidence in medical and psycho-social literature that a multi-faceted approach – from spirituality, to intervention considering trauma and addiction – will prove more effective for women. Alongside the factors named in WIT, as people of faith the Church sees Christianity as a foundational organizing principle in life. The Christian faith is incarnational, taking seriously the particular contexts and experiences of individuals, while inviting those individuals into a journey of faith and eschatological narrative. Covington's recognition from a secular standpoint of the importance of spirituality in recovery is an open door through which the Church might offer theological content to this claim and expand its meaning and potential efficacy. This is not new to the recovery movement; rather, spirituality has long been considered central to recovery for mutual-aid approaches such as the 12-step programme, which derived its approach from the Christian tradition. There are natural synergies between Covington's WIT and the relational approach of L'Arche that might begin a fruitful conversation around how the Church might build community with women experiencing addiction. These communities, undergirded by a rich theology of friendship and belonging, might serve as both preventative and rehabilitative spaces. They might both resist the oppressive context of a society in which both social housing and addiction treatment services budgets are not sufficient, and seek instead to provide communities that promote human flourishing. Following Covington's insistence on a systems approach to addiction, it is crucial too that we recognize the impact that housing policy has had on women experiencing addiction. A lack of appropriate housing provision – and cuts to drug and alcohol services, along with domestic violence support – has a direct impact on the welfare of women experiencing addiction and at risk of experiencing it.

Lessons in Building Friendship, Mutuality and a More Human Society from L'Arche and Others in the Field

L'Arche defines its mission as to 'create communities with a culture of shared lives between people with and without intellectual disabilities, from which we can work together to build a more human society'. Members identify that 'mutual relationships and trust in God are at the heart of our journey together' and 'celebrate the unique value of every person and recognize our need of one another'.[18] Rich theological themes are present here that might help us in developing a culture for a community of women with and without experience of addiction living together. They might also aid us in speaking theologically into the housing crisis more broadly, prioritizing the consideration of every individual with dignity and agency. Exploring all of them is beyond the remit of this chapter; however, it is worth touching on two elements that particularly resonate and further elucidate Covington's approach: first, Christian friendship and mutuality and, second, building a more human society.

Christian Friendship and Mutuality

> The L'Arche Relational Model breaks down barriers between those who give and those who receive support. It replaces society's emphasis on independence that leaves so many people lonely, with interdependence where each person flourishes as they contribute their gifts for the good of others.[19]

On first reading, there might not seem to be anything that is distinctive about this approach, but in fact it runs contrary to the conventional model of ministry and social engagement. Samuel Wells, theologian, vicar and friend of L'Arche, describes 'working for' as the norm, where 'one person has a need, while the other person has skills, availability, and willingness to help'.[20] This model has strong parallels with medical models of disability and addiction where doctors and therapists seek to 'fix' the patient in an unintegrated manner. There is a danger that in so doing the individual concerned is disempowered and too closely identified with their condition. L'Arche models an approach that is quite different, choosing instead to create a space in which all can be with God and with one another. Wells writes that 'being with' is focused on 'companionship', warning that 'sometimes the obsession with finding solutions can get in the way of forming profound relationships of mutual understanding, and sometimes relationships are more significant than the solutions'.[21] It is this sense of mutuality – of sharing life together and recognizing the gifts of each individual – between those with disabilities and those without – that creates a sense of genuine community at L'Arche and promotes human flourishing. Concurrently, it is through this 'mutual care, respect and compassion' that those with and without disability 'reach their full potential'.[22] The subtle shift here is of profound significance: in the words of John Swinton, Chair of Divinity and Religious Studies at the University of Aberdeen, 'they do not live together as carer and cared for but as fellow human beings who share care and need'.[23] Friendship is key to the formation of a community that is no longer providing services but building homes together.

In our professionalized, medico-psychiatric world, it may seem naïve to consider friendship a tool for the liberation of the oppressed – or support for those with addictions – yet if we look to the biblical narrative, we see that Jesus approached his ministry with an attitude of friendship. He sought friendship with the tax collector, the sinner, the drunkard and the glutton (Luke 7.34; Matt. 11.19); he befriended those who were excluded from society. Relationships are considered central to recovery by Covington as well: she considers PTSD as a 'disease of disconnection' and suggests that creating a safe environment for relationships to be built is crucial. Importantly, this engagement with friendship is not a denial of the importance of expertise; rather, while specialized care remains proficient, it is not sufficient. Specialist care for women experiencing addiction is crucial but necessarily complemented – as WIT highlights – by safe community, strong relationships and a growing sense of self apart from the addiction. Within our society where care of the marginalized is often professionalized, the concept of friendship is both necessary and radical in seeing the person amid the diagnosis. In the context of considering how the Church treats those with schizophrenia, Swinton considers friendship to be a powerful force for the reclamation of the centrality of the person; friendship is focused on the individual rather than the illness or other stigmatizing label attributed to an individual. This refocusing on personhood is equally powerful for women with addictions, who face a higher level of stigma and shame than men.[24] L'Arche develops a community that resists this stigmatization through mutuality and respect. Swinton sees this form of Christian friendship directed towards 'those whom society rejects and marginalizes'[25] as a radical act that recognizes our common humanity, is willing to transcend the boundaries society has enforced around difference, and with a desire to heal the fragmentation that has led to the oppression of many. It is an intentional posture that, 'inspired by the power of the spirit, takes its shape from the relationships of Jesus the Messiah, and seeks to embody and act out something of his life and purpose'.[26]

What does this look like? Once again, the answer is both

simple and profound. While the way people live together in L'Arche is not prescribed, there are some common features that are recognizable, including the value of eating together, shared times of prayer and reflection, honest communication and a willingness to accompany and celebrate one another. L'Arche assistants (those who do not have disabilities) are not expected to be expert in any of the disabilities core members (those with disabilities) have or provide specialist care, but to grow in friendship and build a supportive environment that cultivates a sense of belonging. Often more experienced assistants will take leadership roles within each L'Arche house, along with core members who are willing and able. A similar pattern might emerge in our proposed residential community, where healthy relationships and rhythms might be developed to provide supportive environments for those in recovery. The needs of women will vary, and those who require specific therapeutic intervention would be able to access professional support. Similarly, women without addictions would not be expected to have a particular expertise, but could be supported with ongoing training and supervision while resident in the community. L'Arche communities are often formed by a number of houses with 6–12 residents in each, encouraging participation, allowing flexibility and fostering relationships. These communities, undergirded by a rich theology of friendship and belonging, might serve as both preventative and rehabilitative spaces that offer safe, secure housing for women with addictions who are either at risk of, or have experienced, homelessness, alongside other women who have not.

One practical model that is growing traction in the UK housing market that prioritizes participation of residents in housing developments is Community Led Housing (CLH). While there are multiple models of CLH which might be appropriate, the cohousing model fits most naturally with this imagined community. Cohousing is an approach to creating community involving the built environment and participation of residents to build a neighbourhood that embodies particular values. As CLH describes itself, 'these values are generally linked to a shared vision for living in a certain way'[27] that promotes human flourishing for those involved. This is a holistic model that resists the commodification of housing, prioritizing community building that is highly participatory, involving all potential residents as key decision makers in both the design of the build and the ongoing aspects of the community. Cohousing communities can both exist in new-builds and re-purposing of existing buildings, but always prioritize forming housing that promotes intentional community, with shared spaces and facilities, tailored for the particular needs and desires of the community. Here we have a model that would both empower women who are often given passive roles in their housing to be actively involved in the process, ensuring their voices are heard and needs accounted for, while providing an intentional community focused around the particular mission we have described.

Considering this concept of mutual friendship in the context of a residential community of women with addictions and those without, we might begin to imagine a home that is safe, therapeutic and growing for all those involved. For the woman experiencing addiction, she is provided with secure housing, in a safe, female-only environment, where she can develop healthy relationships, belong and begin to imagine again, while the women without are similarly served by this home, these relationships and encounters. In terms of housing needs, it is not simply those experiencing addiction that are supported; there are currently 500,000 more people aged between 20 and 25 living at home with their parents than in 1996[28] as a result of the unaffordability of both private rentals and mortgage deposits and payments. This route might also allow young adult women affordable and secure accommodation. As Victor Hinojosa writes, L'Arche is in many ways a simple project, but one with a radical vision:

> Well beyond making accommodations in existing social structures for those with disabilities . . . [they] have in mind a fundamentally new set of social arrangements with a radical inclusion of the stranger – in this case those with disabilities – which more faithfully models the radical hospitality of the God incarnate in Jesus Christ.[29]

It is to this that we might aspire, seeking to build a community that is radically inclusive of women experiencing addiction in a way that is supportive, dignifying and relational.

Building a More Human Society

L'Arche states its mission as twofold: both to create communities of human flourishing and to challenge societal norms that disadvantage people with disabilities – recognizing that while an impairment is biological, disability is the cumulative disadvantage disabled people experience because of the way that society is designed. Concerning housing, the message in this chapter is also twofold. I have sought to construct a theological and social-scientific justification for creating stable housing for women with and without addiction living together, recognizing the particular gift that Christian friendship undergirded by mutuality might offer both populations. I also hope to have shown that both addiction and homelessness are conditioned by social contexts that make one vulnerable, create stigma and complicate recovery. As addiction theologian Sonia Waters writes, we must 'pay attention, not just to the person, but to the systems of oppression in which they are situated' to best understand the causes of addiction and the routes out.[30] Therefore, we shall now turn to the housing crisis more broadly conceived through the lens of women's experiences.

While this chapter has focused on a particular demographic, it is clear that the L'Arche model has broader application than its original context and might issue in some wider principles for good housing and good community. The relational model of L'Arche might well serve the wider population in promoting human flourishing through a person-centred approach to housing policy that prioritizes the safety and security of residents. In 2016, the UK housing charity Shelter conducted research on the hunt for what 'home' means, with a desire 'to build a common understanding that home is bigger than bricks and mortar'.[31] They identified five aspects to 'home': affordability, decent conditions, space, stability and neighbourhood. In the approach of this chapter, we have primarily focused on the less material aspects of what a home might be, rather than on the 'bricks and mortar'. For women experiencing addiction, the majority of whom have experienced some form of violence, often in the home, the significance of stability and safety are crucial. It is vital that any approach to housing that the Church chooses to take is participatory in nature, giving both agency and security to its inhabitants. It must resist the commodification of housing, reducing homes to units to be sold, ignoring the vital role families and communities play in shaping our societies. The Christian faith resists this, as does the relational model of L'Arche, which prioritizes both the sanctity of individuals and specific values of place. As part of its vision, L'Arche prioritizes engaging with and serving its local neighbourhood, recognizing the incarnational nature of Christian faith.

Too often, conversations around housing talk about the most vulnerable members of society as problems to be solved, cast in purely passive roles. The 'homeless', 'domestically abused' and 'addicted' are talked about as demographics, but rarely spoken with as individuals surviving affliction. Often, organizations that were established to 'help' can employ managerial language that reduces their human agency and suggests that social care can be reduced to an efficient process that ignores the particularity of every person. People are referred to as 'clients' or 'service users', 'addicts' or 'homeless people' and their individual experience is often reductively categorized into 'high-' or 'low-' support needs to be serviced either by support workers or online. Those who have experienced homelessness or addiction face increased barriers to getting a home, and private landlords are less likely to accept new tenants who are claiming benefits. This denigration that is mainstream in the housing market, excluding some of the most vulnerable from stable accommodation, denies the human dignity of those affected. The Gospels paint a different picture, with Jesus befriending, listening to and learning from those who are often outcast by mainstream society. May we learn from the Messianic model, and L'Arche's example of advocacy and solidarity, by putting those on the margins at the forefront of conversation around housing and communities, giving them agency in the development of both housing policy and the homes that they live in. May the Church seek out and hear the voices of those so often ignored, recognizing that the lack of attention to their needs and desires has contributed to the current housing crisis we are facing. It is crucial that women who have experienced addiction and homelessness are treated with human dignity and solidarity, and the gifts of wisdom they have to offer are received. The Church might learn from L'Arche and model a different way that is fitting to its vocation and recognizes that every person is a child of God with unique gifts, and is worth being respected and having their voice listened to.

Conclusion

We are in the midst of a housing crisis decades in the making. It is a crisis that goes beyond bricks and mortar, affecting the physical, emotional and spiritual wellbeing of millions across the UK. As with many crises, it is those with low incomes and facing multiple disadvantage who are hit the hardest. One such demographic, as I have made clear, is women experiencing addiction. It is clear that insecure – or a lack of – housing can be a contributing factor in both the emergence of addiction and a barrier to recovery from it. Safety is crucial for women's recovery, particularly as a result of the relationship between abuse and addiction, and housing is a fundamental aspect of establishing that safety. Any response that is to be sufficient to such an endemic challenge must be holistic in nature, recognizing the role of spirituality in seeking to build homes rather than merely houses, with a focus on community-building and support for its residents. It must also be willing to challenge the flaws in the current housing system that lead to the denigration of citizens and fail to support those most in need. L'Arche does not have the monopoly on Christian community that seeks to be radically hospitable and build a culture of mutuality. Places such as the Pilsdon Community[32] and Windsor Hill Wood[33] also draw on the rich Christian tradition of hospitality to offer a home to those who are struggling and would benefit from a place to belong. I have sought to offer here a picture of what the Church's response might look like, seeking to imagine an incarnational vision of life, inspired by Jesus' ministry, calling us to be present with God and with one another. I have done so in conversation with L'Arche, who have built residential communities with those with disabilities in 38 different countries. Each country will have its own particular housing needs and policies, and no one L'Arche community will look the same. Yet principles of human dignity, mutuality and belonging pervade them all, creating communities that resist the degradation of vulnerable populations in society.

It is crucial that while we seek to create radical visions of Christian community with those on the margins that we challenge the injustices present in the current system. While this chapter proposes a particular example of how women with and without addictions might live together that is workable, albeit with more detail needed around the form of housing/ tenancy and the training involved, the undergirding principles of L'Arche have lessons for the housing crisis more broadly. With a preferential option for the poor, it is crucial the Church attends to the cries of injustice that are so easily left unheard, taking seriously the affliction of those marginalized in society. Through the lens of Christian friendship and mutuality, which sees the person clothed with dignity rather than diagnosis, might the Church offer a loving response that disrupts the current models of housing that leave the vulnerable with precarious housing or none at all, and instead promote their participation in providing solutions to the current crisis. Learning from L'Arche, we might pursue an approach to housing policy that does not ignore the present power disparities, prioritizes the needs of the vulnerable and gives voice to those so often ignored, together building a more human society.

Notes

1 Grierson, J. (2020), 'Domestic Abuse Killings "More than Double" amid Covid-19 Lockdown', www.theguardian.com/society/2020/apr/15/domestic-abuse-killings-more-than-double-amid-covid-19-lock down (accessed 15.4.20).

2 Hauerwas, S. (2008), 'Abled and Disabled: The Politics of Gentleness', *The Christian Century*, 125(24).

3 Tuffrey-Wijne, I. (2020), *How to Share Bad News of Abuse by Someone You Trusted?*, www.tuffrey-wijne.com/?p=767 (accessed 24. 2.20).

4 L'Arche Canada, *The L'Arche Relational Model*, www.larche.ca/en/the-l-arche-relational-model (accessed 25.4.20).

5 L'Arche, *Relational Model*.

6 L'Arche, *Relational Model*.

7 Harvey, S., Mandair, S. and Holly, J. (2013), *Case by Case: Refuge Provision in London for Survivors of Domestic Violence who Use Alcohol and other Drugs or Have Mental Health Problems*, London: EVA Women's Aid and Solace Women's Aid.

8 Office for National Statistics (2019), *Deaths Related to Drug Poisoning in England and Wales: 2018 Registrations*, www.ons.gov. uk/peoplepopulationandcommunity/birthsdeathsandmarriages/deaths/bulletins/deathsrelatedtodrugpoisoninginenglandandwales/2018registrations (accessed 29.2.20).

9 Grierson, J., Hill, A. and Brooks, L. (2019), 'Fears of Public Health Emergency as Drug Deaths Hit Record Levels', www.theguardian.com/society/2019/aug/15/drug-poisoning-deaths-in-england-and-wales-at-highest-level-ever-recorded (accessed 25.4.20).

10 O'Neil, A. L. and Lucas, J. (2015), *Promoting a Gender-responsive Approach to Addiction*, Turin: UNICRI Publication.

11 Harvey, Mandair and Holly, *Case*.

12 Office for National Statistics, *Deaths*.

13 Office for National Statistics, *Deaths*.

14 Fitzpatrick, S. and colleagues (2019), 'The Homelessness Monitor: England', London: Crisis.

15 Solace Woman's Aid (2019), *Safe as Houses: How the System is Failing Women and Children Fleeing Abuse in London*, www.solacewomensaid.org/sites/default/files/2019-10/Solace_SafeasHouses-Report_FINAL_0.pdf (accessed 10.4.20), p. 5.

16 Covington, S. S. (2008), 'Women and Addiction: A Trauma-informed Approach', *Journal of Psychoactive Drugs*, 40(5), p. 381.

17 An alternative, complementary approach is the successfully piloted 'Housing First' approach advocated by Crisis: www.crisis.org.uk/ending-homelessness/the-plan-to-end-homelessness-full-version/solutions/chapter-9-the-role-of-housing-first-in-ending-homelessness/.

18 L'Arche International, www.larche.org/.

19 L'Arche Canada, *Relational Model*.

20 Wells, S. and Owen, M. A. (2011), *Living Without Enemies: Being Present in the Midst of Violence*, Downers Grove, IL: IVP Books, p. 26.

21 Wells and Owen, *Living*.

22 L'Arche International, www.larche.org/.

23 Swinton, J. (2008), 'Introduction: Living Gently in a Violent World', in Hauerwas, S. and Vanier, J. (2008), *Living Gently in a Violent World: The Prophetic Witness of Weakness*, Downers Grove, IL: IVP Books, p. 17.

24 Raine, P. (2018), *Women's Perspectives on Drugs and Alcohol: The Vicious Circle*, New York: Routledge.

25 Swinton, J. (2000), *Resurrecting the Person: Friendship and the Care of People with Mental Health Problems*, Nashville, TN: Abingdon Press, p. 9).

26 Swinton, *Resurrecting*, p. 39.

27 Community Led Homes (2018), *What is Cohousing?*, www.communityledhomes.org.uk/what-cohousing (accessed 1.2.20).

28 Office for National Statistics, *Deaths*.

29 Hinojosa, V. J. (2018), 'From Access to Communion: Beyond the Social Model', *Journal of Disability & Religion*, 22(2), p. 206.

30 Waters, S. E. (2019), *Addiction and Pastoral Care*, Grand Rapids, MI: Eerdmans, p. 20.

31 Shelter (2016), *Living Home Standard*, www.shelter.org.uk/__data/assets/pdf_file/0011/1287848/living_home_standard_full_report.pdf (accessed 12.3.20).

32 Pilsdon Community, *The Pilsdon Community, Sharing a Life of Prayer, Hospitality and Work*, www.pilsdon.org.uk (accessed 23.4.20).

33 Jones, T. (2016), *A Place of Refuge: An Experiment in Communal Living – The Story of Windsor Hill Wood*, London, Riverrun, www.windsorhillwood.co.uk (accessed 23.4.20).

Community, Hospitality and Space-making

NICOLA HARRIS AND JEZ SWEETLAND

Human beings were created for connection – connection to God and to one another. 'Our neural, hormonal and genetic makeup support interdependence over independence . . . we're a social species. That's why connection matters.'[1] Connection is the very fabric of community and brings a sense of belonging. Humans need to be connected to others to thrive and so need community to thrive. This is seen in the needs of a newborn baby; the simple act of receiving milk is not enough. Babies who do not experience connection with a loving adult are likely to experience attachment problems that lead to a variety of lifelong learning and social difficulties.

This need for connection does not end when physical maturity is reached; it continues throughout our lives. The effect of disconnection, or loneliness, on our physical wellbeing has been researched by developmental psychologist Susan Pinker. Bringing together her own research and that of others, she argues that loneliness is literally killing people. She explains, 'loneliness drives up the cortisol and blood pressure levels that damage the internal organs in both sexes, and at all ages and stages of adult life'.[2]

As connection and community are basic human needs essential to our physical and emotional wellbeing, it follows that these would be the primary concerns when building or buying homes. But this is not currently the case. Instead, for some, houses are not homes but assets to accumulate, while others are left without. The negative repercussions of our current housing system are no longer going unnoticed. *The Economist* has been speaking out: 'Housing policies have made the system unsafe, inefficient and unfair. Time to tear down this rotten edifice and build a new housing market that works.'[3] Society needs homes and communities that actively facilitate the potential for connection and community for all.

But even if the availability and affordability housing crisis were solved overnight, many areas of our society still need to embrace a fresh perspective on facilitating the spread of healthy connection within communities. There are different reasons that prevent many from reaching out to new neighbours, perhaps perpetuating neighbourhood cultures where people live physically close, but emotionally distant. In contrast, new neighbours could be welcomed with a knock on the door, a friendly hello or a welcome card. This invites new residents into a culture they are more likely to perpetuate themselves. Both scenarios can take place independently of the type of housing, because it is ultimately the people who maintain a culture of community, not the buildings.

There is a strong pull to remain comfortable and safe in our homes and churches, reinforced and justified by our societal norms and fears of the unknown 'other'. However, that is not the journey of radical discipleship that Jesus invites us on. Christians are called to live by faith and not by fear, demonstrate the extravagant welcome and hospitality of God, even when this impacts on our homes and our places of worship.

Living this way can be messy. One husband and wife interviewed made significant changes to their property to make room for a homeless friend to stay in between his months in rehabilitation for PTSD. When asked about taking risks with those on the fringes of society, they said, 'Our theology suddenly becomes very gritty, which is what it is. These things are not glossy. The reality of these things is that they mess with systems, they mess with procedures, they mess with our stability. Working with people on the fringes is messy and, as a church, that's what we're called to.'

The effects of choosing to reach out to others will be different from one person to another, as each accepts the invitation of Jesus Christ. This chapter explores a few of the ways God has been expressing hospitality: on a personal level through extreme radical hospitality of adoption; moving to a new housing estate, seeking to demonstrate the unconditional love of God; and, finally, a dynamic project on an organizational level. All of these stories express God's people seeking to reach out to connect and create community, to enable a sense of belonging, and express practically the love and welcome of God.

Community

'Community' is a wonderfully broad term, hard to define yet easy to experience. As Pinker argued, when living in a healthy community, humans are affected by the warmth, connection, security and constructive tension of others in their lives. Feelings of isolation or a lack of control of circumstances can lead to feelings of disconnection; these can dehumanize and negatively affect wellbeing.

Interestingly, in a widely celebrated TED Talk from 2015 titled 'Everything You Think You Know About Addiction is Wrong', British journalist Johann Hari explores the underlying causes of addiction and concludes that the opposite of addiction is not sobriety, but connection. This conclusion resonates with Pinker's argument; we are designed for connection and the loss of connection has significant consequences:

The Victorians understood this. Sociologists and politicians rediscovered it in the 1980s when they asked why huge programmes of welfare had not conquered poverty. That was when they began to realize that social problems often have a personal, psychological and communal dimension as well as an economic one. We need networks of support. Without them people feel vulnerable and alone, and it is hard to solve personal crises alone.[4]

When considering the shared church experience, terms such as 'church community' or 'church family' are often used. They confidently express our choice of togetherness, shared values and commitment to one another. Of course, even in church communities there can be isolation, disconnection and disagreement.

In part, it was desire for authentic community that led Jez and Jo Sweetland, with their young family, to set up and live in an intentional community home in Bristol for six years. This was a desire to make more sense of their own Christian faith, to have a lived expression of that faith. Going to church a little more regularly and swearing a little less than many of their professed non-Christian friends did not provide for Jez and Jo a great enough evidence to the truth and power of a life transformed in Jesus. After all, part of the journey of the Christian faith is an invitation to a greater awareness of our communion with God, while including an invitation to relinquish control.

With trepidation, naivety and excitement, shaped on loosely formed plans, the Sweetlands journeyed into intentional community living. On reflection, this journey would require more of them than they anticipated but the adventure of faith proved to be an invitation into deeper connection and a richer life for them. In taking up the invitation to relinquish control they learnt to live and thrive in the 'fullness' and 'messiness' of life.

They were particularly inspired by the early Church as expressed in Acts:

All the believers were one in heart and mind. No one claimed that any of their possessions was their own, but they shared everything they had. With great power the apostles continued to testify to the resurrection of the Lord Jesus. And God's grace was so powerfully at work in them all that there was no needy person among them. For from time to time those who owned land or houses sold them, brought the money from the sales and put it at the apostles' feet, and it was distributed to anyone who had need. (Acts 4.32–34)

The simple ambition of Jez and Jo was to learn to live more generously and to create an extended family home. This focused around three key elements: shared meals (collective food shopping and evening meals cooked and eaten together), intentional shared time as a household (establishing a rhythm of time together to facilitate connections with one another), and shared possessions (a nine-bedroom home was fully furnished with the intention that all possessions were shared). The home was set out in the same way that many of us would hope for a family home: more of 'ours' than 'mine'.

The relational and lived experience within the Sweetland household was ever changing, both in terms of people and location, and the community moved from a Bristol townhouse to a rural farmhouse after five years. Extended 'family' members changed regularly, ranging from 0–63 years old, and at its fullest they had 13 people living as family under one roof. The loss of control and the mess was very real, but so was life. They celebrated four weddings as community members moved into their own new family homes and it was encouraging to Jez and Jo to think that community living and this wider family experience did not put people off marriage!

It was not always easy. During the Sweetlands' first year they describe the experience as 'like looking in a mirror that rather unkindly highlights all your "faults" . . . We had preferred to think of ourselves as generous, easy going, forgiving; we found out that those characteristics are easily challenged when control and our preferred order were taken away . . . There were also the challenges of dealing with irreconcilable differences, poorly communicated or misaligned expectations and retaining healthy family boundaries for the marriage and the nuclear family.'

Some of those challenges proved to be hard and painful lessons for all involved; partly as these dynamic and complex personal situations were worked out in the community home. On a couple of occasions, this resulted in people electing to leave, or being invited to leave, the community for the benefit of themselves and the remaining family. Those experiences were painful and disappointing for all, but also left a legacy of experience about navigating hurt, the need for brave communication, and the need to communicate and review expectations around trust and leadership with clear alignment to responsibility and ownership. Forgiveness was always an integral part of the journey.

The Sweetlands found that community living offered an invitation to be that 'work in progress' the gospel describes and to be known and loved despite failings. On their wall hangs a quote by Shane Claiborne from his powerful book *Irresistible Revolution*, 'May we catch each other with grace when we fall short of who we want to be.'[5]

The community evolved to have an open-door policy, welcoming friends and neighbours to join the rhythms of the household who journeyed as a family underpinned by a shared Christian faith. The community created a safe place of belonging, to equip and encourage one another to share God's wisdom and love in whatever area of society they lived and worked in. They gathered around the belief that everyone is a work in progress; needing connection to shape and encourage us in our faith, grow our vision, deepen our identity, and hear God for each other. We are all made uniquely in God's image and each of us has something powerful to reveal about God's character.

Ultimately, that part of the Sweetlands' adventure ended in 2018 when their landlord put the house up for sale and they could not find an alternative to house the entire community. Despite efforts to find another large house to rent to relocate the community, and even an attempt to co-purchase a hotel, no alternative community home could be found, and the community agreed to disband, continuing to maintain close friendships.

The Sweetland family moved to a rented terrace house and the other community members moved into other house shares or set up smaller community homes. 'We are aware how the friendships and the shared experiences have shaped all involved. The commitment, cost and value of investing to create intentional community has marked us. We are now more aware of how a commitment to community can be expressed in so many different ways and we have the opportunity to learn a new expression in a more typical setting.' They now look to build community and connection in their own streets, bringing lessons from the community house to a different type of community, and building that 'extended family' culture with others.

Jez and Jo dream of returning to community living and they continue to prayerfully pursue this, as their experience as a family was rich and real. On reflection, Jez and Jo say they lived a 'life-changing experience'. They learnt how community can positively shape us but how, equally, it will cost us. From their experience, the price is a sound investment; it deepens faith, lovingly exposes character flaws that need redemption, and builds healthy and resilient connection.

Their lives and expression of faith continue to be shaped by their experience of community, and by a growing compassion for those who, as a result of the housing crisis, do not have a secure home and are without hope that they will ever have a place to call home. Jez and Jo were so impacted by the reality of the housing crisis that in 2017 Jez gave up his job in law to work in partnership with others to set up the Bristol Housing Festival.

This five-year Festival launched in October 2018 and is committed to acting as a catalyst for change in the area of housing, primarily focusing on two elements:

- First, supporting and enabling an increase in housing supply by creating healthy public/private collaborations to deliver sustainable homes by deploying off-site technology (often referred to as modern methods of construction, or MMC).
- Second, looking at how off-site housing technology can help cities build the houses they really need; including a focus on building healthy and resilient communities, and celebrating success stories with a focus on how lives are positively impacted.

It is critical that as new housing is built, there is a focus on the importance of building community.

It is the people that make and support the culture of a community, not the physicality of the built environment. Certainly, it is true that well-designed spaces can enable community. It is also possible, no doubt, to think of 'awful' places that have rich and vibrant community and other 'well-designed' spaces that feel disconnected and lifeless. It is the complexity of people, with strongly held views, oddly formed habits and the ability to display irrational or deliberately hurtful behaviour, that makes community so vital and yet so challenging and risky. Housing is relatively straightforward until you involve people!

A shared narrative is needed to build hope for what's possible across all sectors of society: national government, industry, politicians and the local community. Arguably, it will take an army to build real and lasting change. The Church is well equipped and well placed to help support that necessary change with a community ready and placed to serve in each neighbourhood.

Those who make up the Church are called to be light to the world, to fulfil the great commission to go and make disciples of all nations. There is an invitation to seek, to pray and intervene, so God's compassion, generosity and justice affect the current housing market's systemic failure. There are questions to be wrestled with: how is the Church called to live counter-cultural lives that powerfully demonstrate the values of God's kingdom and the command to love our neighbour as ourselves? For those with homes and assets, how can the parable of the talents challenge and inspire radical stewardship? How can the Church courageously give away, share and build community?

This will look different from person to person, community to community, as the Holy Spirit leads – the concept of community can be expressed in a million different ways and the list is not close to being exhausted. In community, the creativity and multiplicity of God can be so wonderfully expressed, but at its heart is the invitation to us all into a great adventure of faith, to co-labour in building community and connection, demanding that the Church is led by Christ and willing to pay a price to love and serve, to model a different kind of kingdom expressing the heart of our loving God.

We see something of the Church taking up this invitation in the case studies that follow: God's unconditional and radically generous love being freely available and experienced in different homes and communities. These offer a variety of expressions of community, each with the pursuit of expressing God's heart at the centre, despite the mess and the hardship involved.

It appears that this is the nature of journeying with God into learning to love him and others more deeply:

> To love at all is to be vulnerable. Love anything and your heart will be wrung and possibly broken. If you want to make sure of keeping it intact you must give it to no one, not even an animal. Wrap it carefully round with hobbies and little luxuries; avoid all entanglements. Lock it up safe in the casket or coffin of your selfishness. But in that casket, safe, dark, motionless, airless, it will change. It will not be broken; it will become unbreakable, impenetrable, irredeemable. To love is to be vulnerable.[6]

Notes

1 Brown, B. (2017), *Braving the Wilderness*, New York: Random House Books.

2 Pinker, S. (2015), *The Village Effect: Why Face to Face Contact Matters*, London: Atlantic Books.

3 *The Economist* (2020), 'The Horrible House Blunder: Why the Obsession with Home Ownership is so Harmful', *The Economist*, 16 January.

4 Sacks, J. (2007), *The Home We Build Together*, London: Continuum Books, p. 131.

5 Claiborne, S. (2006), *The Irresistible Revolution: Living as an Ordinary Radical*, Grand Rapids, MI: Zondervan.

6 Lewis, C. S. (1960), *The Four Loves*, London: Collins Fontana Books.

CASE STUDIES – HOUSING AND COMMUNITY

Case Study One: The Radical Hospitality of a Lifelong Welcome

The Revd Dr Helen Collins, member of faculty at Trinity College, Bristol, gave a lecture in January 2020 on 'Political: Migration and Housing' to those training for ordained church leadership. In this lecture, Helen briefly spoke of how wrestling with theology of housing led her and her husband on a journey to the radical and costly hospitality of adoption.

Following her own theological studies at Trinity College, Helen, her husband and two young children were offered a curacy house that seemed perfect and she could picture it as 'home'. However, this offer fell through, and instead they went to live in a larger house that was draughty, cost a fortune to heat, and had no immediate neighbours nearby to help them feel they belonged. Reflecting on God's purposes in the house change, they sought to use the extra space to host meals for larger groups, guests at Christmas and, latterly, the 17-year-old daughter of friends, who lived with them for a year. This was, in Helen's words, 'really good and really challenging'.

Their thoughts of hospitality led to considering fostering and then adoption. Knowing they would be moving house soon after the adoption took place, they needed to demonstrate to the authorities that they could provide stability and a support network for the new member of their family. Helen spoke in the adoption interviews of the Church and its role as an extended eschatological family. Therefore, they argued, wherever they ended up living, they would be part of their local church and this community.

A year after their adopted son, Arthur (name changed), came to live with them, they moved house, joined their local parish church, and made connections there and within the wider community. They chose to both sow into the community and reap the benefits of knowing others and being known, of belonging somewhere. But this was not, and is not, easy: Arthur has additional needs, as is so often the case with children who have gone through trauma. Helen says 'he is known in the community, but so also is his occasionally challenging behaviour! Thankfully, there's an acceptance that comes with that knowledge and people seem really fond of him.' Helen continued, 'The localness of community, the day-to-day support, walking past each other's houses, has become essential to family life in general but especially when there are the additional challenges.'

These challenges are 24/7, as many parents of children with additional needs will know. 'Today I was recording a lecture. It was interrupted by a noise so I stopped, and went downstairs and Arthur was having a full-on meltdown as he was tired and frustrated that he couldn't have a sticker. I had to help support my other children while my husband calmed him down. I quickly had a sandwich and then came to work for a break! That's every day, there's no escape, no let up, and it's really difficult to call on others for help. But knowing God's resourcing in it all, knowing that it's OK to not cope, to say: "We don't even know how to do this and we're probably doing this really badly . . ." He teaches me probably more than anything else the limits of my own capacity, otherwise I'd probably be tempted to think that my capacity is endless, I'm omnicompetent – Arthur is constantly reminding me that it's only by God's grace that any of us do anything . . .'

Helen described how their initial narrative during the adoption process was how they could give a home to someone who would not otherwise have one. But this started to shift as the process continued, becoming about how they could be all that God intended them to be through the gift of welcoming another into their home. 'He saves us from middle-class perfectionism and achievement, having it all together, pretending everything is fine . . . our adopted son is a gift to us that is making us more whole than we would otherwise be.'

Helen was asked what this journey has taught them about the kingdom of God. 'I said in the adoption process that I believe that in the new creation we will love everyone as we currently love our nearest and dearest – our whole concept of family will be redefined, and everybody will be our brothers and sisters in Christ for eternity. So, we'd better get practising for what that means now in terms of loving the other we didn't choose, or choosing to love the other.'

Helen and her family's journey with Arthur is both inspiring and challenging. It is inspiring because reaching out to fully embrace and welcome someone unknown into their home speaks so loudly of the love and generosity of God, and challenging because it is extremely costly and uncomfortable. As Helen says: 'It's flipping hard work, but transformation is.'

Case Study Two: Finding God in a New Community

The Revd Ali Boulton was in the monthly Baptist Minister's Prayer Meeting on 17 January 2008 when she first heard of the new housing development being built on the southern outskirts of Swindon. As they bowed their heads to pray for the development, Ali unexpectedly met with God in a way that would guide the path she and her husband, Neil, took from that point on.

God made it very clear to Ali that he wanted the Boulton family to move on to this new estate, a financial impossibility for them at that time. But others caught the vision, some generously contributing to the purchase of their new home, and three other couples from Ali and Neil's home group also feeling called to buy homes there too. Ali looks back at this as the 'team' who were the start of their church community, The Stowe, which later became a gathered church community.

In April 2009, the Boulton family moved into the first house on the enormous development that continues to be built in 2020. Impacted by the financial crash of 2008, many other private buyers had pulled out of their house purchases, giving the Boultons a month to settle into their new home with no neighbours to meet – but God, as ever, had a plan.

Ali had attended every community meeting concerning the new estate prior to moving in. John, a Citizen Housing Association worker (name changed), 'found out that there was a crazy lady moving in and he searched me out!' Citizen Housing was providing the social housing on the development, housing that made up one-third of the new estate. John and Ali built up a friendship. A community group called The StoweAway was formed, with the first contribution from Citizen Housing, and the welcome for the new residents was planned. They used their influence to ensure that Ali was invited to council and other stakeholder meetings. This triggered a friendship with David and Rachel (names changed) from the council project team. The social housing provider became keen to support Ali's work in the new community, as were, increasingly, the council project team.

With very few private buyers moving in alongside the Boulton family, the next wave of new residents to move on to the estate filled the social housing and each new household was welcomed by a smiling Ali and a welcome basket alongside the housing officer with the house key. This basket represented the strong sense Ali had that they were called to bless the new residents unconditionally, without any other agenda. It contained a box of teabags, a jar of coffee, a bag of sugar, a light bulb, washing-up liquid, a J-cloth, a toilet roll and binbag, along with the council sustainability information, and ('bravely or stupidly', as she puts it) Ali's contact details. Every basket was gratefully received. Ali explained that she was their neighbour and also a Baptist minister, but 'we're here to serve all faiths or none. What shall we do to make this a good community? If you want to get in touch, then do.'

Initially those who got in touch asked for practical help: the state-of-the-art fibre-optic provision to each new home meant that familiar ways of connecting with TV and internet were rendered obsolete and people asked Ali for help. She and Neil would visit the homes, with IT-whizz Neil sorting their TV connections, and Ali conversationally building on the connection made with the welcome baskets.

Equipped with all she had learnt through the community meetings, Ali was aware that the Boulton family's move into the first house triggered the initial Section 106* requirements, which

---

*The Section 106 agreement is a legal contract that developers make with

would be essential to those moving there, especially those without a car: 'All of these lovely people were moving in, on a slightly out-of-town estate, with no facilities [shops or a school] . . . but we moved in a month before, which triggered the 106 requirement of a bus service.' As a resident and because of her growing relationship with the council, Ali was able to lobby for this provision, along with the triggering of new postcodes for the area.

There were significant problems obtaining home insurance as the estate was built on a floodplain and, 'once one insurance company turns you down, they all do'. Ali was able to work with the Baptist Insurance by explaining the situation, and also with the Environment Agency to get the relevant documents on record, including a 1,000-year flood plan, enabling other residents to get their home insurance too. Working on all these very practical issues was a way to serve their neighbours as Ali and Neil had felt called to do.

'One of the first big calls we had was straight after Community Day [a village fete-type event] and someone called as she was about to kill herself. She had two children in the car. She said, "I know you're a vicar and you believe in God and maybe there is a God, can you help me?" I went and talked with her and my kids looked after her kids – thankfully she didn't kill herself.' Since this incident, Ali has been on mental health first aid training as well as being involved with other neighbours who have been suicidal.** And more conversations about God have come about, initiated by the neighbours themselves.

In 2010, the public gathering of The Stowe began, requested by a neighbour unconnected to the church; this was another way in which God spoke to the team through the community. Ali does not pretend that it has been easy – seeing resolution in some challenges over the years, but not yet in others. She

---

the council planning authority. The agreement ensures that there is funding for appropriate community infrastructure (bus services, etc.) to be in place both to serve the new community and to reduce the impact of the new housing on the existing community.

**For statistics on suicide, see the Mental Health Foundation (2019), *Mental Health Statistics: Suicide*, Mental Health Foundation, www.mentalhealth.org.uk/statistics/mental-health-statistics-suicide (accessed 24.6.20).

gives the example of times of conflict between others in the neighbourhood, ending up being the one hated in the middle: 'Working on a business model, I'd have been far better to have taken sides in a conflict because then you keep all the people on one side, and lose the other side, but at least you keep half the people. But what happens when you say God has called me to love both of you?'

Ali explained how it costs to accept God's invitation to seek to be Jesus and see Jesus in the lives of their neighbours. 'It costs to accept this invitation to choose to love and be loved, intentionally sharing our lives, and at times our homes, with neighbours – not just those with seemingly "simple" lives. It's been a massive discipleship journey of laying down my life, that's the underlying thing. What does it mean to lay down the right to privacy in my house? What does it look like when I lay down that I only really want people to see my house when it's in a tidy and presentable state, not the "lived-in" look? What does it look like for people to turn up at my house in crisis, stay overnight and shout? What does it look like when we have someone who is homeless on and off, and people blame me for his behaviour because he is living in my house? What does it mean to genuinely love everybody?'

She is inspired by the apostles' lifestyle of having 'everything in common' (Acts 2.44). This has led to some radical sharing of resources, including finance and housing costs. Recently, during the lockdown due to the coronavirus pandemic, they have seen this generosity of spirit extend out, with others beyond The Stowe willingly sharing with others. Ali said, 'We're running a food bank in my hallway and my co-minister's garage! It's done through friendship and we call them "hampers". We're using the language of *sharing*, not *giving*, in the community. We try to be generous and give people what they would like as well as simply what they need, as this reflects the nature of who God is. We give people treats, nice things, praying over the hampers for guidance to give people something that *they'd* like.'

They have been able to share with some who are used to working and paying for their needs themselves, but have been unable to do so due to a lack of work and income. As well as sharing food, Ali has bought treatments in advance to support a local beautician: 'I've only had beauty treatments since I moved here: it's a great relationship builder!' It's another very practical way to show love and support in this community.

Five years after moving in, as Ali's ministry expanded, The Stowe called on the help of co-minister the Reverend Owen Green. This highlighted the importance of together articulating the underlying DNA values of the mission and ministry. The core Stowe community seek to live out and disciple one another in these values – they seek to have an attitude of Christ.

Alongside her life on the estate, Ali now spends time encouraging others to missionally engage in new housing areas through her work with the New Housing Hub. She encourages others to contextualize God's good news on their estates, training them by using these seven underlying principles:

- Bless unconditionally.
- Live incarnationally.
- Listen to God and the community, hearing God through the voice of the community.
- Be friends.
- Lay down your life.
- Lay down your agenda for what gathered church is.
- Keep going.

The New Housing Hub's vision is 'to work together [across denominations and traditions] to love every new community'. Ali expands on this: 'Really my heart is that we would work together to love *every* community. I don't think we *bring* God, I think he's already here. That is evident because we've heard God through non-Christians in our community, so God is clearly here. It's not about *bringing* God's love but embodying his love as authentically as we can, with all our limitations because we're all on a discipleship journey, aren't we?'

Case Study Three: A Local Partnership for an Intentional Community

The YMCA hostel, The Wing, in Bristol is a beautiful historic building, a lovingly restored police headquarters. The work and money put into its renovation was very intentional: '[it] ascribes value to the young people: they are worth putting into a nice building rather than just a purely functional place'. These are the words of Ben Silvey, Director of YMCA Bristol, who was instrumental in The Wing's development and subsequent opening in January 2018.

The young people, or 'residents', Ben speaks of are those in housing crisis who stay in nine of the 90 hostel beds to provide them with a 'breathing space' for an average three-month stay. The other 81 beds in the hostel are used by commercial guests and enable the residents to stay in the hostel independent of council or government funding, contributing financially if they are able. This gives a flexibility that would otherwise not be possible. The team believe strongly in not stigmatizing the young people, so it is not generally possible to tell who a resident is and who is a commercial guest.

Ben goes further in describing this core element to The Wing as a breathing space for the young people: 'There's a very stressful element to something that's happened to them before they end up in housing crisis. So, we wanted to create something of a breathing space, a moment where they could stop, have a bit of time to take the pressure off, and work out what's next.'

Facilitating this breathing space is not simply about the beautiful building and the value it demonstrates to the residents. Two chaplains, Nikki and Julia, are employed, and Ben describes their input as key to making The Wing work for the young people who reside there for a season.

A large part of their role is facilitating community within The Wing, encouraging connections and a sense of home. The 'cornerstone' of this sense of community is 'The Feast', a meal that takes place every Thursday at 6 p.m. to which anyone in the building is invited – to help prepare or simply enjoy. 'Sometimes there are three people, sometimes 43 . . . the point is, it's a place where everyone is just a human being. They're not a traveller, they're not a member of staff, they're just people sharing a meal together.' It may sound very simple, but Ben describes how the simplicity works and they see the residents grow in their inter-actions with others. This is the centre point of the community at The Wing.

Ben Silvey and Jez Sweetland first connected before the Bristol Housing Festival was formulated, sharing an experience of com-munity living and both looking to express their love for God and his kingdom through their different involvement in the city.

Ben was already seeing that the current move-on accom-modation for their residents was not satisfactory for their needs, and was exploring options with housebuilding companies. 'We wanted to create for young people not just institutional relation-ships, not just key workers, housing workers, support workers and youth workers . . . we wanted to create friends, neighbours and community so that when a young person moves on, they still have this network of people who they have lived alongside, who are not bound by professional boundaries . . . community living could do that.'

Through this organic connection between Ben and Jez, once the Bristol Housing Festival was launched and sites for new modular housing were being considered, a partnership developed between the YMCA, the Bristol Housing Festival, Bristol City Council and ZEDPods (a low carbon modular housing solution), leading to a housing development pilot in Bristol that was fit-tingly called 'Hope Rise'.

Hope Rise is a collection of 11 homes, nine of which have one bedroom, with two houses on either end that have two bedrooms. These off-site manufactured homes will be council housing, but specifically allocated to young people, five through the council's Home Choice system and four nominated through The Wing. These young people will be able to remain in these homes for around two years, encouraged and supported during their time to find more mainstream housing. Should they be unable to find suitable accommodation after two years, they will not be evicted, but will be supported further until a new home is found.

Knowing that creating a good community culture needs to be done intentionally, the other two homes, at either end of Hope Rise, will be occupied by specifically recruited 'community builders' who will get all the benefits of being council tenants in exchange for simply being good neighbours – catalysts for community activity and a bridge between the YMCA and the Hope Rise Community, supported by the team at The Wing.

This project and The Wing are a response to the desperate situation for young people when it comes to finding an affordable place to live, alongside the recognition that houses themselves do not make homes. Ben believes 'life works better when we're part of a community . . . generally speaking, we're more resilient in life, life is fuller, when we have people around us who care for us.'

Ben believes many young people are suffering because of the injustices of our current housing system: rising house prices – and, consequentially, high rents – mean that even some working young people cannot afford to rent a room in a house and are, therefore, more vulnerable to homelessness. For Ben, this is a place for Christians to partner with God: 'We are clearly called to serve the poorest people and to create a more just society, and those two things have come together in trying to do housing differently.' Working towards providing truly affordable homes for these young people in a positive community is an expression of the kingdom of God, and the hope and our prayer is that they experience life in the Hope Rise Community in a way that enables them to live there – and then leave there – as people who know they can connect and belong in a community because they are valued as human beings.

These case studies show us that creating a life-giving home and community is far from easy and it means that those involved lean heavily on Jesus, picking up their cross each day, and walking with him. These are just a few responses to the incredible mandate of the Church to 'love your neighbour', to demonstrate the love of God by sharing, practically loving those in need, and meeting people where they are and *where we are*. This is our mandate to build communities of hope.